Cuisinart Griddler Cookbook for Beginners 2021

1001-Day Newest Perfect Cuisinart Griddler Recipes for Tasty Backyard BBQ to Feed Your Family and Friends

Loryd Robince

© Copyright 2021 Loryd Robince - All Rights Reserved.

In no way is it legal to reproduce, duplicate, or transmit any part of this document by either electronic means or in printed format. Recording of this publication is strictly prohibited, and any storage of this material is not allowed unless with written permission from the publisher. All rights reserved.

The information provided herein is stated to be truthful and consistent, in that any liability, regarding inattention or otherwise, by any usage or abuse of any policies, processes, or directions contained within is the solitary and complete responsibility of the recipient reader. Under no circumstances will any legal liability or blame be held against the publisher for any reparation, damages, or monetary loss due to the information herein, either directly or indirectly.

Respective authors own all copyrights not held by the publisher.

Legal Notice:

This book is copyright protected. This is only for personal use. You cannot amend, distribute, sell, use, quote or paraphrase any part of the content within this book without the consent of the author or copyright owner. Legal action will be pursued if this is breached.

Disclaimer Notice:

Please note the information contained within this document is for educational and entertainment purposes only. Every attempt has been made to provide accurate, up-to-date and reliable, complete information. No warranties of any kind are expressed or implied. Readers acknowledge that the author is not engaging in the rendering of legal, financial, medical or professional advice.

By reading this document, the reader agrees that under no circumstances are we responsible for any losses, direct or indirect, which are incurred as a result of the use of information contained within this document, including, but not limited to, errors, omissions, or inaccuracies.

Table of Contents

Introduction 5
Chapter 1: Meet the Cuisine Art GR 5 in 1 Griddler 6
    Benefits of 5 in 1 Cuisine Art GR Griddler 6
Chapter 2: How to Use the Griddler 8
    Setting up the Plates 8
    Instructions Manual 9
    Cleaning and Maintenance 10
    FAQs 10
Chapter 3: Panini and Eggs Recipes 12
    Sausage Scrambled Eggs 12
    Breakfast Panini 13
    Italian Panini 14
    Vegan Scrambled Eggs 15
    Spinach Scrambled Eggs 16
    Scrambled Eggs and Cheese 17
    Chocolate Panini 18
    Bacon, Tomato and Cheddar Panini .. 19
    Mexican Scrambled Eggs 20
    Basic Grilled Panini 21
Chapter 4: Pancake and Waffle Recipes 22
    Peanut Butter Pancakes 22
    Raspberry Pancakes 23
    Blueberry Cream Cheese Pancakes 24
    Almond Butter Pancakes 25
    Double Chocolate Pancakes 26
    Chocolate Waffles 27
    Blueberry Waffles 28
    Cinnamon Pancakes 29
    Morning Waffles 31
    Cheddar Cheese Pancakes 32
    Red Velvet Pancakes 33
    Pumpkin Cream Cheese Pancakes 34
    Walnut Pumpkin Pancakes 35
Chapter 5: Poultry Recipes 36
    Yucatan Chicken Skewers 36
    Lemon Grilled Chicken Thighs 38
    Grilled Duck Breasts 39
    Grilled Chicken Skewers 40
    Chicken Burgers 41
    Tequila Chicken 42
    Grilled Chicken Breast 43
    Grilled Honey Chicken 44
Chapter 6: Beef, Pork and Lamb Recipes 45
    Greek Souzoukaklia 45
    Margarita Beef Skewers 47
    Cheese Burgers 48
    Sweet Ham Kabobs 49
    Grilled Pork Chops 50
    Salisbury Steak 52
    Teriyaki Beef Skewers 53
    Chimichurri Beef Skewers 54
    Flank Steak 56
    Grilled Lamb with Herbes De Provence
    58
    Raspberry Pork Chops 59
    American Burger 60
    Fajita Skewers 61

    Honey Glazed Pork Chops 62
    Grilled Lamb Chops 63
    Lamb Skewers 64

Chapter 7: Seafood Recipes **66**
    Pistachio Pesto Shrimp 66
    Grilled Garlic Scallops 68
    Blackened Salmon 69
    Lemon-Garlic Salmon 70
    Shrimp Skewers 71
    Ginger Salmon 72
    Barbecue Squid 74
    Salmon Lime Burgers 76

Chapter 8: Vegetable Recipes **77**
    Cauliflower Zucchini Skewers 77
    Tarragon Asparagus 78
    Butter Glazed Green Beans 79
    Cauliflower Steaks 80
    Grilled Veggies with Vinaigrette 82
    Grilled Veggies 84
    Grilled Mushroom Skewers 85
    Grilled Butternut Squash 86
    Grilled Brussels Sprouts 87
    Grilled Eggplant 88
    Grilled Zucchini 89
    Veggie Burger 90

Chapter 9: Dessert Recipes **92**
    Grilled Apples 92
    Rum-Soaked Pineapple 93
    Cinnamon Grilled Peaches 94
    Banana Butter Kabobs 95
    Marshmallow Stuffed Banana 96
    Marshmallow Roll-Up 97
    Fruit Kabobs 98
    Apricots with Brioche 99

Conclusion **100**

Introduction

This cookbook is not just for the Cuisinart Griddler, but just about any indoor grill, George Foreman Grill, Hamilton Beach Indoor Flavor/Searing Grill. Preparing low-carb, high-carb, and high-protein meals at home has never been faster or more delicious!

This is a comprehensive cookery book that will guide you on how to operate the Cuisinart Griddler and prepare delightful meals on it. you to create more memories with your Griddler and your new recipes.

Whether you are cooking for one or the whole family, these mouth-watering recipes grill recipes are crowd-pleasers. You will find commonly used ingredients in the recipes, so when you shop at the grocery store, you'll know exactly what to buy.

Chapter 1: Meet the Cuisine Art GR 5 in 1 Griddler

Cuisine GR Griddler is another name for convenience, and it works best for those who love to enjoy a variety of grilled food at home, but they are too busy to set up an outdoor grill. It has made indoor grilling in an electric griller super simple, easy, and affordable. It is simple to manage and control. What makes the Cuisine GR Griddler stand apart from other electric grills is the basic design and user-friendly control it provides. The ceramic coated grilling plates with a flat side to cook other types of meals make cooking an effortless experience. And this cookbook tells you how exactly this griddle is going to meet all your grilling needs and to help you cook an entire menu. But before we get to that, let's have a look at some of the benefits this Griddler offers to its users:

Benefits of 5 in 1 Cuisine Art GR Griddler

Following are a few of the known benefits that an electric grill like that of Cuisine GR Griddler guarantees to provide:

1. **Temperature Control**

   The function of the thermostat is to keep the internal temperature of the Griddler. As with charcoal or outdoor grills, we need to maintain it manually with a constant check, whereas in an electric griddle like this, the thermostat does that temperature controlling for us. As soon as the appliance is heated to the required temperature, you will see the change of color on the knob of its respective cooking plate, which indicates that you can start cooking.

2. **Safe and User Friendly**

   The wiring and heating elements in this Griddler are completely insulated, and the entire unit is protected with a solid layering on the outside. The plates do not move until their button is pressed to push them out. The flip lid is adjustable and can be kept in an open position by using the lever that is attached inside. The knobs are given at the bottom of the part, which is insulated, and that gives a safe control.

3. **Double-Sided Plates**

   The Griddler offers a variety of cooking options because it comes with a double-sided cooking plate. One-sided of plates can be used to grill food, and the other side is kept non-stick with a flat surface to cook food like pancakes or egg scrambles, etc. This means that a user can cook a variety of meals using this single device.

4. **No Pollution**

No smoke, no grease, no woodchips, no coal, just a portable Griddler that can be used inside the kitchen and can be kept in a shelve once it is cleaned. So, this appliance allows fuss-free and mess-free cooking every time.

5. Easy for Beginners

Grilling outdoor or in any other complicated grilling appliance is never easy for beginners; it always takes experience and time to get to understand the rules of grilling and setting up the right temperature, but now with electric griddle like Cuisine GR Griddler, even beginners can cook and grill a variety of food at home.

Chapter 2: How to Use the Griddler

The advanced multifunctional 5 in one Cuisine GR Griddler has made grilling an effortless experience. Who knew indoor grilling would become so easy? But now Cuisine GR has introduced its multipurpose Griddler, which allows you to grill, and roast, and cook different food items. The device with three knobs to control its cooking operations. And each package comes with two non-stick multi-purpose plates.

When you unbox the appliance, you will find two Griddler and grilling plates along with the base unit. The base unit is an insulated vessel which has a flip lid attached to one side of the base. When you open the lid, there is a heating element inside, which is covered with removable cooking plates.

Outside the base unit, there is a panel with three control knobs:

1. Griddle: This knob is used to set the temperature for the bottom plate. The temperature for this knob is mentioned in Fahrenheits, ranging from 200 to 420 degrees F.
2. Selector: This knob lets you select whether you want to use one plate or both plates. To heat and use only the BOTTOM plate, turn the knob to the "Griddle" position. And to use both plates, turn the knob to the "Grill Panini" position.
3. Grill panini: This knob lets you select the temperature for the upper plate. The temperature ranges from WARM, LOW, MED, HIGH, and SEAR.

Setting up the Plates

The advantage of using the removable two side plates is that you can fix and remove any according to the need of the recipe. Here is how you can set the plates in different combinations:

1. Half Griddle: To use this appliance as a half griddle, heat the bottom side of the appliance after fixing the bottom plate with its flat side up.
2. Full Griddle: To use it as a full griddle, open up the lid and fix it by pulling the lever on the side. Insert the plates on sides of the Griddler with their flat side up.
3. Half grill: To do so, use the only lower side of the Griddler and insert the bottom plate with its grilling surface upward.
4. Full grill: To do so, use both sides of the Griddler, keep the lid flat opened, fix it and insert both plates in their respective positions with their grilling surface upward.
5. Half grill-half griddle: You can also use it in this way, keep the lid flat opened, fix it and insert one plate with its flat surface upward and insert the second plate with its grilling surface facing outside.

Instructions Manual

To use the cuisine Art Griddler up to its potential, here is how you can cook using this appliance:

1. First, set up the appliance on a sturdy surface, on which you will have enough space to keep its lid flat open. It is best to on the open countertop, away from other appliances.
2. Plugin the appliance. Since it is not an automatic Griddler, you will need to set the temperature to initiate preheating manually.
3. If you are using the appliance for the first time, make sure to wash its plate and dry them before putting them to use.
4. To remove the plates from their position, press the button given on the side of each plate and pull the plates out of their grooves.
5. Check if the dripping plate is set in its place and if it is completely empty.
6. To put the plates back into their place, simply press them into their grooves until they are fixed.
7. Once the plates are set in place according to the requirement of the recipe, the step is preheating.
8. Use the selector knob to choose one plate cooking or two plates cooking, as described in the previous section. Select "griddle" for one plate cooking and "grill panini" for two plates cooking.
9. Then select the temperature for each plate by using their respective knobs: Griddle knob for bottom plate and Grill Panini knob for the upper plate.
10. Close the lid for now and let the machine preheat. The light on the knobs changes their colors when it is preheated.
11. Add food and cook in the Griddler according to the recipe.
12. Remember that the lights on the knobs keep changes when you cook food in the Griddler with its lid flat open because the temperature keeps changing in opening cooking. Don't get confused or distracted; it's normal, and you should continue cooking without disturbing the temperature settings in such a case.

Cleaning and Maintenance

The best part about this Griddler is that it is super easy to clean. As soon as you remove and detach the plates from the appliance, you can clean them without damaging the machine. Both the plate of the cuisine GR Griddler is 100 percent dishwasher safe, so you can wash them easily in the dishwasher, or you can wash them with soap water. Avoid scratching the plates with hard scrubbers as it may damage the non-stick coating.

1. After you are done cooking, unplug the Cuisine GR Griddler and allow it to cool down completely. The hot plates might cause the burn, so only remove them from Griddler after 20-25 minutes of cooking.
2. Leave the lid open when the device is cooling down. It is best to keep the lid in the open flip position. This helps you to remove the upper and lower plates easily.
3. Now press the buttons that are given on the sides of the Griddler, and that will detach the plates from their base. Now you can remove the plates easily by pulling them out.
4. Take the scraper that comes with the appliance and scrape off the hard food particles that are stuck to its surface. If the particles are too stick, soak the plates in soap water for 5 minutes, then scrap them to clean.
5. You can also use baking soda and water to clean the plate.
6. Drizzle baking soda and water over the sticky food particles or grease, leave it for 5 minutes then wipe it off.
7. When the food particles are removed, simply wash both sides of the plate using soap water and a soft sponge.
8. Allow the plate to dry completely before putting them back inside the Griddler.
9. There is a dripping tray under the bottom part of the Griddler, which can be pulled out from the back. This tray catches all the grease and excess liquid. Remove this tray after a cooking session and rinse and wash it thoroughly then insert it back into its plate before the next session.
10. Clean the base unit from the inside and the outside using a lightly wet cloth.
11. Do not immerse or wash the base unit or the lid with water.

FAQs

1. **Can I use any other steel or iron plates to cook in this Griddler?**

No, the double sides multipurpose plates that come with this cuisine Griddler are specifically designed for the appliance, and they fit rightly on top of the heating elements. Other plates might not fit in their place, and they will not give the desired results. However, you can always use the Cuisine Art Waffle plates, which can be bought separately.

2. **Can you cook liquid food in the Cuisine GR Griddler?**

No, Cuisine GR Griddler is only designed for grilling and roasting purposes; cooking liquid food is not suitable since the plates can't carry enough space.

3. Is it necessary to preheat the Cuisine GR Griddler before cooking?

Yes, the appliance takes its time to reach the required temperature at which you want to cook the food. Cooking without preheating might affect the cooking time or the texture of the food that is cooked.

Chapter 3: Panini and Eggs Recipes

Sausage Scrambled Eggs

Preparation Time: 10 minutes
Cooking time: 5 minutes
Serving: 3

Ingredients:

- 3 eggs
- ¼ cup milk
- Black pepper, to taste
- 2 ounces bulk pork sausage
- 2 bacon slices, chopped
- ¼ cup cooked ham, diced

Method:

1. Beat eggs with milk, black pepper, pork sausage, and bacon in a bowl.
2. Open the top lid of the Cuisine Griddler and set the flat plate sides up.
3. Turn the "Selector" knob to the "Grill Panini" side.
4. Preheat the bottom plate of Cuisine Griddler at 350 degrees F and the upper plate on medium heat.
5. Once it is preheated, pour the egg mixture on both plates.
6. Stir and cook the eggs for 5 minutes until set.
7. Serve warm.

Nutritional Information per Serving:

- Calories 224
- Total Fat 16.4g
- Saturated Fat 5.4g
- Cholesterol 202mg
- Sodium 652mg
- Total Carbs 2g
- Fiber 0.2g
- Sugars 1.3g
- Protein 16.4g

Breakfast Panini

Preparation Time: 10 minutes
Cooking time: 5 minutes
Serving: 2

Ingredients:

- 3 teaspoons butter
- 1 scrambled egg
- 2 slices Italian sandwich bread
- 1 (3/4-ounce) slice Deli American
- 2 (1-ounce) slices ham

Method:

1. Brush the top of one bread slice with butter.
2. Add scrambled egg, deli American and ham slices on top.
3. Place another bread slice on top.
4. Cut the sandwiches into half diagonally and brush the top with butter.
5. Turn the "Selector" knob to the "Grill Panini" side.
6. Preheat the bottom grill of Cuisine Griddler at 350 degrees F and the upper grill on medium heat.
7. Once it is preheated, place the sandwiches in the grill.
8. Close the griddler's lid and grill the panini for 5 minutes.
9. Serve warm.

Nutritional Information per Serving:

- Calories 233
- Total Fat 16.1g
- Saturated Fat 7.4g
- Cholesterol 235mg
- Sodium 676mg
- Total Carbs 7.5g
- Fiber 0.6g
- Sugars 0.9g
- Protein 13.8g

Italian Panini

Preparation Time: 10 minutes
Cooking time: 5 minutes
Serving: 6

Ingredients:

- 1 loaf rustic Italian bread, sliced
- 4 teaspoons honey mustard
- 12 ounces provolone sliced
- 4 ounces Black Forest ham, thinly sliced
- 4 ounces roast turkey breast, thinly sliced
- 4 ounces Genoa salami, thinly sliced
- 3 tablespoons butter, softened

Method:

1. Place half of the bread slices on the working surface and brush the top with butter.
2. Divide the honey mustard, provolone, ham, turkey, salami over the bread slices.
3. Set the remaining bread slices on top of the salami.
4. Cut the sandwiches into half diagonally and brush the top with butter.
5. Turn the "Selector" knob to the "Grill Panini" side.
6. Preheat the bottom grill of Cuisine Griddler at 350 degrees F and the upper grill on medium heat.
7. Once it is preheated, place the sandwiches in the grill.
8. Close the griddler's lid and grill the panini for 5 minutes.
9. Serve warm.

Nutritional Information per Serving:

- Calories 424
- Total Fat 30.2g
- Saturated Fat 16.5g
- Cholesterol 104mg
- Sodium 1449mg
- Total Carbs 8.8g
- Fiber 0.4g
- Sugars 1.2g
- Protein 28.5g

Vegan Scrambled Eggs

Preparation Time: 10 minutes
Cooking time: 8 minutes
Serving: 4

Ingredients:

- 1 package medium tofu, crumbled
- ¼ cup nutritional yeast
- 2 teaspoons garlic powder
- ½ teaspoons turmeric
- 1 teaspoon black salt
- ½ teaspoons black pepper
- 1 cup chicken broth

Method:

1. Blend yeast, garlic powder, turmeric, black pepper, salt, broth in a blender.
2. Pour this mixture into a bowl and stir in crumbled tofu, then mix well.
3. Turn the "Selector" knob to the "Grill Panini" side.
4. Open the top lid of the Cuisine Griddler and set the flat plate sides up.
5. Preheat the bottom plate of Cuisine Griddler at 350 degrees F and the upper plate on medium heat.
6. Once it is preheated, add the tofu mixture to both plates.
7. Stir and cook the tofu mixture for 8 minutes until set.
8. Serve warm.

Nutritional Information per Serving:

- Calories 73
- Total Fat 2.3g
- Saturated Fat 0.5g
- Cholesterol 0mg
- Sodium 783mg
- Total Carbs 6.7g
- Fiber 3.1g
- Sugars 0.7g
- Protein 8.7g

Spinach Scrambled Eggs

Preparation Time: 10 minutes
Cooking time: 5 minutes
Serving: 6

Ingredients:

- 2 oz full-fat yogurt
- 1 tablespoon olive oil
- 1 cup spinach, chopped
- 6 large eggs
- ⅓ cup cheddar cheese, shredded

Method:

1. Beat eggs with olive oil, spinach, cheddar cheese, and yogurt in a bowl.
2. Open the top lid of the Cuisine Griddler and set the flat plate sides up.
3. Turn the "Selector" knob to the "Grill Panini" side.
4. Preheat the bottom plate of Cuisine Griddler at 350 degrees F and the upper plate on medium heat.
5. Once it is preheated, pour the egg mixture on both plates.
6. Stir and cook the eggs for 5 minutes until set.
7. Serve warm.

Nutritional Information per Serving:

- Calories 124
- Total Fat 9.4g
- Saturated Fat 3.2g
- Cholesterol 193mg
- Sodium 118mg
- Total Carbs 1.7g
- Fiber 0.1g
- Sugars 1.2g
- Protein 8.3g

Scrambled Eggs and Cheese

Preparation Time: 10 minutes
Cooking time: 5 minutes
Serving: 2

Ingredients:

- 2 large eggs
- 2 tablespoons milk
- 1/8 teaspoon cayenne pepper
- 1/4 teaspoon salt
- 1 scallion, thinly sliced
- 2 tablespoons cheddar cheese, shredded
- 1 cherry tomato, quartered

Method:

1. Beat eggs with milk, cayenne pepper, salt, scallion, cheddar, and tomato in a bowl.
2. Open the top lid of the Cuisine Griddler and set the flat plate sides up.
3. Turn the "Selector" knob to the "Grill Panini" side.
4. Preheat the bottom plate of Cuisine Griddler at 350 degrees F and the upper plate on medium heat.
5. Once it is preheated, pour the egg mixture on both plates.
6. Stir and cook the eggs for 5 minutes until set.
7. Serve warm.

Nutritional Information per Serving:

- Calories 117
- Total Fat 7.7g
- Saturated Fat 3.2g
- Cholesterol 195mg
- Sodium 413mg
- Total Carbs 2.9g
- Fiber 0.6g
- Sugars 2.3g
- Protein 8.7g

Chocolate Panini

Preparation Time: 10 minutes
Cooking time: 5 minutes
Serving: 4

Ingredients:

- 4 challah bread slices
- 2 ounces semisweet chocolate, chopped

Method:

1. Place the 2 bread slices on the working surface and top the bread with chocolate.
2. Set the remaining bread slices on top and press gently.
3. Cut the sandwiches into half diagonally.
4. Turn the "Selector" knob to the "Grill Panini" side.

Preheat the bottom grill of Cuisine Griddler at 350 degrees F and the upper grill on medium heat.

5. Once it is preheated, place the sandwiches in the grill.
6. Close the griddler's lid and grill the panini for 5 minutes.
7. Serve warm.

Nutritional Information per Serving:

- Calories 281
- Total Fat 10.9g
- Saturated Fat 5.4g
- Cholesterol 0mg
- Sodium 327mg
- Total Carbs 44.1g
- Fiber 3.8g
- Sugars 19.9g
- Protein 5.7g

Bacon, Tomato and Cheddar Panini

Preparation Time: 10 minutes
Cooking time: 5 minutes
Serving: 4

Ingredients:

- 1 ½ tablespoons butter, softened
- 4 sourdough bread slices
- 4 Colby-Jack cheese slices
- 4 large tomato slices
- 4 cooked bacon slices

Method:

1. Place half of the bread slices on the working surface and brush their top with butter.
2. Divide the bacon, tomatoes, and cheese slices on top of the bread slices.
3. Set the remaining bread slices on top of the cheese.
4. Cut the sandwiches into half diagonally and brush the top with butter.
5. Turn the "Selector" knob to the "Grill Panini" side.
6. Preheat the bottom grill of Cuisine Griddler at 350 degrees F and the upper grill on medium heat.
7. Once it is preheated, place the sandwiches in the grill.
8. Close the griddler's lid and grill the panini for 5 minutes.
9. Serve warm.

Nutritional Information per Serving:

- Calories 233
- Total Fat 12.9g
- Saturated Fat 5.5g
- Cholesterol 32mg
- Sodium 678mg
- Total Carbs 18.3g
- Fiber 0.8g
- Sugars 0.8g
- Protein 10.9g

Mexican Scrambled Eggs

Preparation Time: 10 minutes
Cooking time: 5 minutes
Serving: 4

Ingredients:

- 2 tablespoons vegetable oil
- 1 tomato, roughly chopped
- 1 spring onion, chopped
- 1 green chili, chopped
- 4 large eggs, beaten
- ¼ teaspoon Maldon salt

Method:

1. Beat eggs with vegetable oil, tomato, spring onion, green chili, and Maldon salt in a bowl.
2. Open the top lid of the Cuisine Griddler and set the flat plate sides up.
3. Turn the "Selector" knob to the "Grill Panini" side.
4. Preheat the bottom plate of Cuisine Griddler at 350 degrees F and the upper plate on medium heat.
5. Once it is preheated, pour the egg mixture on both plates.
6. Stir and cook the eggs for 5 minutes until set.
7. Serve warm.

Nutritional Information per Serving:

- Calories 138
- Total Fat 11.8g
- Saturated Fat 2.9g
- Cholesterol 186mg
- Sodium 101mg
- Total Carbs 1.8g
- Fiber 0.3g
- Sugars 1.1g
- Protein 6.5g

Basic Grilled Panini

Preparation Time: 10 minutes
Cooking time: 5 minutes
Serving: 4

Ingredients:

- 1 tablespoon olive oil
- 2 Italian bread slices
- 2 tablespoons mayonnaise
- 2 Cheddar cheese slices
- 3 deli ham slices
- 1 tomato slice
- 1 onion slice

Method:

1. Place one bread slice on the working surface and brush their top with mayo.
2. Add ham, tomato, onion, and cheddar cheese on top of the bread.
3. Set the other bread slice on top of the cheese.
4. Cut the sandwich into half diagonally and brush the top with butter.
5. Turn the "Selector" knob to the "Grill Panini" side.
6. Preheat the bottom grill of Cuisine Griddler at 350 degrees F and the upper grill on medium heat.
7. Once it is preheated, place the sandwiches in the grill.
8. Close the griddler's lid and grill the panini for 5 minutes.
9. Serve warm.

Nutritional Information per Serving:

- Calories 164
- Total Fat 12.6g
- Saturated Fat 4.5g
- Cholesterol 29mg
- Sodium 443mg
- Total Carbs 5.6g
- Fiber 0.5g
- Sugars 0.8g
- Protein 7.5g

Chapter 4: Pancake and Waffle Recipes

Peanut Butter Pancakes

Preparation time: 5 minutes
Cooking time: 4 minutes
Servings: 4

Ingredients:

- 1 egg, beaten
- ½ cup Mozzarella cheese, shredded
- 3 tablespoons granulated Sugar
- 2 tablespoons peanut butter

Method:

1. Turn the "Selector" knob to the "Griddle" side.
2. Preheat the bottom plate of the Cuisine GR Griddler at 350 degrees F.
3. In a medium bowl, put all ingredients and with a fork, mix until well combined.
4. Pour ¼ of the mixture into preheated Griddler and cook for about 2 minutes per side.
5. Cook for pancakes using the remaining batter.
6. Serve warm.

Nutritional Information per Serving:

- Calories 145
- Total Fat 11.5 g
- Saturated Fat 3.1 g
- Cholesterol 86 mg
- Sodium 147 mg
- Total Carbs 33.6 g
- Fiber 1 g
- Sugar 1.7 g
- Protein 8.8 g

Raspberry Pancakes

Preparation time: 10 minutes
Cooking time: 4 minutes
Servings: 2

Ingredients:

- 1 egg, beaten
- 1 tablespoon cream cheese, softened
- ½ cup Mozzarella cheese, shredded
- 1 tablespoon powdered sugar
- ¼ teaspoon raspberry extract
- ¼ teaspoon vanilla extract

Method:

1. Turn the "Selector" knob to the "Griddle" side.
2. Preheat the bottom plate of the Cuisine GR Griddler at 350 degrees F.
3. In a medium bowl, put all ingredients and with a fork, mix until well combined.
4. Pour ½ of the mixture into preheated Griddler and cook for about 2 minutes per side.
5. Cook more pancakes using the remaining batter.
6. Serve warm.

Nutritional Information per Serving:

- Calories 269
- Total Fat 5.2 g
- Saturated Fat 2.5 g
- Cholesterol 91 mg
- Sodium 88 mg
- Total Carbs 30.6 g
- Fiber 0 g
- Sugar 0.2 g
- Protein 5.2 g

Blueberry Cream Cheese Pancakes

Preparation time: 10 minutes
Cooking time: 4 minutes
Servings: 2

Ingredients:

- 1 egg, beaten
- 1/3 cup Mozzarella cheese, shredded
- 1 teaspoon cream cheese, softened
- 1 teaspoon all-purpose flour
- ¼ teaspoon baking powder
- ¾ teaspoon powdered sugar
- ¼ teaspoon ground cinnamon
- ¼ teaspoon vanilla extract
- Pinch of salt
- 1 tablespoon fresh blueberries

Method:

1. Turn the "Selector" knob to the "Griddle" side.
2. Preheat the bottom plate of the Cuisine GR Griddler at 350 degrees F.
3. In a bowl, place all ingredients except for blueberries and beat until well combined.
4. Fold in the blueberries.
5. Pour 1/2 of the mixture into preheated Griddler and cook for about 2 minutes per side.
6. Cook more pancakes using the remaining batter.
7. Serve warm.

Nutritional Information per Serving:

- Calories 90
- Total Fat 5 g
- Saturated Fat 2.7 g
- Cholesterol 97 mg
- Sodium 161 mg
- Total Carbs 25.7 g
- Fiber 2.8 g
- Sugar 1.2 g
- Protein 5.7 g

Almond Butter Pancakes

Preparation time: 5 minutes
Cooking time: 4 minutes
Servings: 2

Ingredients:

- 1 large egg, beaten
- 1/3 cup Mozzarella cheese, shredded
- 1 tablespoon sugar
- 2 tablespoons almond butter
- 1 teaspoon vanilla extract

Method:

1. Turn the "Selector" knob to the "Griddle" side.
2. Preheat the bottom plate of the Cuisine GR Griddler at 350 degrees F.
3. In a medium bowl, put all ingredients and with a fork, mix until well combined.
4. Pour ¼ of the mixture into preheated Griddler and cook for about 2 minutes per side.
5. Cook for pancakes using the remaining batter.
6. Serve warm.

Nutritional Information per Serving:

- Calories 253
- Total Fat 12.3 g
- Saturated Fat 2 g
- Cholesterol 96 mg
- Sodium 65 mg
- Total Carbs 13.6 g
- Fiber 1.6 g
- Sugar 1.2 g
- Protein 7.9 g

Double Chocolate Pancakes

Preparation time: 10 minutes
Cooking time: 4 minutes
Servings: 2

Ingredients:

- 2 teaspoons coconut flour
- 2 tablespoons sugar
- 1 tablespoon cacao powder
- ¼ teaspoon baking powder
- 1 egg
- 1-ounce cream cheese, softened
- ½ teaspoon vanilla extract
- 1 tablespoon 70% dark chocolate chips

Method:

1. Turn the "Selector" knob to the "Griddle" side.
2. Preheat the bottom plate of the Cuisine GR Griddler at 350 degrees F.
3. In a bowl, add flour, Sugar, cacao powder and baking powder and mix well.
4. Add the egg, cream cheese and vanilla extract and beat until well combined.
5. Gently, fold in the chocolate chips.
6. Pour ½ of the mixture into preheated Griddler and cook for about 2 minutes per side.
7. Cook more pancakes using the remaining batter.
8. Serve warm.

Nutritional Information per Serving:

- Calories 151
- Total Fat 11.9 g
- Saturated Fat 6.8 g
- Cholesterol 97 mg
- Sodium 76 mg
- Total Carbs 15.9 g
- Fiber 2.8 g
- Sugar 0.3 g
- Protein 5.7 g

Chocolate Waffles

Preparation time: 5 minutes
Cooking time: 6 minutes
Servings: 4

Ingredients:

- ¼ cup all-purpose flour
- 2 tablespoons cocoa powder
- 1 teaspoon baking powder
- 2 tablespoons butter, melted
- 2 large eggs
- 2 ounces melted chocolate
- ¼ cup powdered sugar
- 1½ teaspoons vanilla extract

Method:

1. Turn the "Selector" knob to the "Grill Panini" side.
2. Fix a waffle plates in the cuisine gr Griddler, preheat it at 350 degrees F and preheat the upper plate on medium heat.
3. In a bowl, add the butter and eggs and beat until creamy.
4. Add the cocoa powder, sugar, chocolate, vanilla extract and salt and beat until well combined.
5. Add the flours and baking powder and beat until well combined.
6. Pour ¼ of the mixture into preheated Griddler, close the lid and cook for about 3 minutes.
7. Cook for waffle using the remaining batter.
8. Serve warm.

Nutritional Information per Serving:

- Calories 212
- Total Fat 7.5 g
- Saturated Fat 9.1 g
- Cholesterol 216 mg
- Sodium 167 mg
- Total Carbs 24.1 g
- Fiber 0.2 g
- Sugar 2.1 g
- Protein 4 g

Blueberry Waffles

Preparation time: 5 minutes
Cooking time: 6 minutes
Servings: 4

Ingredients:

- ¼ cup all-purpose flour
- 1 teaspoon baking powder
- 2 tablespoons butter, melted
- 2 large eggs
- 2 ounces blueberry preserves
- ¼ cup powdered sugar
- 1½ teaspoons vanilla extract

Method:

1. Turn the "Selector" knob to the "Grill Panini" side.
2. Fix a waffle plates in the cuisine gr Griddler, preheat it at 350 degrees F and preheat the upper plate on medium heat.
3. In a bowl, add the butter and eggs and beat until creamy.
4. Add the blueberry preserves, sugar, vanilla extract and salt and beat until well combined.
5. Add the flour and baking powder and beat until well combined.
6. Pour ¼ of the mixture into preheated Griddler, close the lid and cook for about 3 minutes.
7. Cook for waffle using the remaining batter.
8. Serve warm.

Nutritional Information per Serving:

- Calories 215
- Total Fat 8.5 g
- Saturated Fat 9.1 g
- Cholesterol 116 mg
- Sodium 131 mg
- Total Carbs 21.6 g
- Fiber 1.1 g
- Sugar 4.7 g
- Protein 3.8 g

Cinnamon Pancakes

Preparation time: 10 minutes
Cooking time: 4 minutes
Servings: 2

Ingredients:

- 1 large egg, beaten
- ¾ cup mozzarella cheese, shredded
- ½ tablespoon unsalted butter, melted
- 2 tablespoons all-purpose flour
- 2 tablespoons sugar
- ½ teaspoon ground cinnamon
- ½ teaspoon psyllium husk powder
- ¼ teaspoon baking powder
- ½ teaspoon vanilla extract

For Topping:

- 1 teaspoon powdered sugar
- ¾ teaspoon ground cinnamon

Method:

1. Turn the "Selector" knob to the "Griddle" side.
2. Preheat the bottom plate of the Cuisine GR Griddler at 350 degrees F.
3. In a medium bowl, put all ingredients and with a fork, mix until well combined.
4. Pour ¼ of the mixture into preheated Griddler and cook for about 2 minutes per side.
5. Cook more pancakes using the remaining batter.
6. Meanwhile, for topping: in a small bowl, mix together the sugar and cinnamon.
7. Place the pancakes onto serving plates and set aside to cool slightly.
8. Sprinkle with the cinnamon mixture and serve immediately.

Nutritional Information per Serving:

- Calories 242
- Total Fat 10.6 g
- Saturated Fat 4 g
- Cholesterol 106 mg
- Sodium 122 mg
- Total Carbs 24.1 g

- Fiber 2 g
- Sugar 0.3 g
- Protein 7.7 g

Morning Waffles

Preparation time: 5 minutes
Cooking time: 6 minutes
Servings: 4

Ingredients:

- ¼ cup all-purpose flour
- 2 tablespoons almond flour
- 1 teaspoon baking powder
- 2 tablespoons butter, melted
- 2 large eggs
- 2 ounces sour cream, softened
- ¼ cup powdered sugar
- 1½ teaspoons vanilla extract
- Pinch of salt

Method:

1. Turn the "Selector" knob to the "Grill Panini" side.
2. Fix a waffle plates in the cuisine gr Griddler, preheat it at 350 degrees F and preheat the upper plate on medium heat.
3. In a bowl, add the butter and eggs and beat until creamy.
4. Add the cream, sugar, vanilla extract and salt and beat until well combined.
5. Add the flours and baking powder and beat until well combined.
6. Pour ¼ of the mixture into preheated Griddler, close the lid and cook for about 3 minutes.
7. Cook for waffle using the remaining batter.
8. Serve warm.

Nutritional Information per Serving:

- Calories 217
- Total Fat 18 g
- Saturated Fat 8.8 g
- Cholesterol 124 mg
- Sodium 173 mg
- Total Carbs 26.6 g
- Fiber 3.3 g
- Sugar 1.2 g
- Protein 5.3 g

Cheddar Cheese Pancakes

Preparation time: 5 minutes
Cooking time: 5 minutes
Servings: 2

Ingredients:

- 1 egg, beaten
- ½ cup Cheddar cheese, shredded
- Pinch of salt

Method:

1. Turn the "Selector" knob to the "Griddle" side.
2. Preheat the bottom plate of the Cuisine GR Griddler at 350 degrees F.
3. Place about 1/8 cup of cheese in the bottom of the Griddler and top with half of the beaten egg.
4. Now, place 1/8 cup of cheese on top and cook for about 5 minutes.
5. Repeat with the remaining cheese and egg.
6. Serve warm.

Nutritional Information per Serving:

- Calories 145
- Total Fat 11.6 g
- Saturated Fat 6.6 g
- Cholesterol 112 mg
- Sodium 284 g
- Total Carbs 30.5 g
- Fiber 0 g
- Sugar 0.3 g
- Protein 9.8 g

Red Velvet Pancakes

Preparation time: 10 minutes
Cooking time: 4 minutes
Servings: 2

Ingredients:

- 2 tablespoons cacao powder
- 2 tablespoons Sugar
- 1 egg, beaten
- 2 drops super red food coloring
- ¼ teaspoon baking powder
- 1 tablespoon heavy whipping cream

Method:

1. Turn the "Selector" knob to the "Griddle" side.
2. Preheat the bottom plate of the Cuisine GR Griddler at 350 degrees F.
3. In a medium bowl, put all ingredients and with a fork, mix until well combined.
4. Pour ½ of the mixture into preheated Griddler and cook for about 2 minutes per side.
5. Cook more pancakes using the remaining batter.
6. Serve warm.

Nutritional Information per Serving:

- Calories 370
- Total Fat 6 g
- Saturated Fat 3 g
- Cholesterol 92 mg
- Sodium 34 mg
- Total Carbs 33.2 g
- Fiber 1.5 g
- Sugar 0.2 g
- Protein 3.9 g

Pumpkin Cream Cheese Pancakes

Preparation time: 10 minutes
Cooking time: 4 minutes
Servings: 2

Ingredients:

- 1 egg, beaten
- ½ cup Mozzarella cheese, shredded
- 1½ tablespoon sugar-free pumpkin puree
- 2 teaspoons heavy cream
- 1 teaspoon cream cheese, softened
- 1 tablespoon all-purpose flour
- 1 tablespoon Sugar
- ½ teaspoon pumpkin pie spice
- ½ teaspoon baking powder
- 1 teaspoon vanilla extract

Method:

1. Turn the "Selector" knob to the "Griddle" side.
2. Preheat the bottom plate of the Cuisine GR Griddler at 350 degrees F.
3. In a medium bowl, put all ingredients and with a fork, mix until well combined.
4. Pour ½ of the mixture into preheated Griddler and cook for about 2 minutes per side.
5. Cook more pancakes using the remaining batter.
6. Serve warm.

Nutritional Information per Serving:

- Calories 110
- Total Fat 7.8 g
- Saturated Fat 3.1 g
- Cholesterol 94 mg
- Sodium 82 mg
- Total Carbs 21.3 g
- Fiber 0.8g
- Sugar 1 g
- Protein 5.2 g

Walnut Pumpkin Pancakes

Preparation time: 10 minutes
Cooking time: 4 minutes
Servings: 2

Ingredients:

- 1 egg, beaten
- ½ cup Mozzarella cheese, shredded
- 2 tablespoons all-purpose flour
- 1 tablespoon sugar-free pumpkin puree
- 1 teaspoon Sugar
- ¼ teaspoon ground cinnamon
- 2 tablespoons walnuts, toasted and chopped

Method:

1. Turn the "Selector" knob to the "Griddle" side.
2. Preheat the bottom plate of the Cuisine GR Griddler at 350 degrees F.
3. In a bowl, add all ingredients except pecans and beat until well combined.
4. Fold in the walnuts.
5. Pour ½ of the mixture into preheated Griddler and cook for about 2 minutes per side.
6. Cook more pancakes using the remaining batter.
7. Serve warm.

Nutritional Information per Serving:

- Calories 148
- Total Fat 11.8 g
- Saturated Fat 2 g
- Cholesterol 86 mg
- Sodium 74 mg
- Total Carbs 23.3 g
- Fiber 1.7 g
- Sugar 0.8 g
- Protein 6.7 g

Chapter 5: Poultry Recipes

Yucatan Chicken Skewers

Preparation Time: 10 minutes
Cooking time: 5 minutes
Serving: 6

Ingredients:

- 6 chicken thighs, boneless, cut in half lengthwise
- 1/2 cup orange juice
- 1/4 cup lime juice
- 2 tablespoons canola oil
- 2 tablespoons ancho chile powder
- 3 garlic cloves, chopped
- 2 tablespoons chipotle in adobo sauce, pureed
- Salt and black pepper, to taste

Method:

1. Mix orange juice, lime juice, canola oil, chile powder, garlic, chipotle, black pepper and salt in a large bowl.
2. Add chicken thighs to the marinade then rub the chicken well.
3. Thread the chicken on the skewers and keep them aside.
4. Turn the "Selector" knob to the "Grill Panini" side.
5. Preheat the bottom grill of Cuisine Griddler at 350 degrees F and the upper grill plate on medium heat.
6. Once it is preheated, open the lid and place chicken skewers in the Griddler.
7. Close the griddler's lid and grill the chicken for 5 minutes.
8. Serve warm.

Nutritional Information per Serving:

- Calories 284
- Total Fat 25 g
- Saturated Fat 1 g
- Cholesterol 49 mg
- Sodium 460 mg
- Total Carbs 35 g
- Fiber 2 g
- Sugar 6 g

- Protein 26g

Lemon Grilled Chicken Thighs

Preparation Time: 10 minutes
Cooking time: 6 minutes
Serving: 4

Ingredients:

- Juice and zest of 2 lemons
- 2 sprigs fresh rosemary, chopped
- 2 sprigs fresh sage, chopped
- 2 garlic cloves, smashed and chopped
- 1/4 teaspoon crushed red pepper
- 4 chicken thighs, trimmed
- Kosher salt, to taste

Method:

1. Rub the chicken thighs with salt, oil, red pepper, garlic, sage, rosemary, lemon zest and juice.
2. Place the chicken in a bowl, cover and marinate for 1 hour for marination.
3. Turn the "Selector" knob to the "Grill Panini" side.
4. Preheat the bottom grill of Cuisine Griddler at 350 degrees F and the upper grill plate on medium heat.
5. Once it is preheated, open the lid and place 2 chicken thighs in the Griddler.
6. Close the griddler's lid and grill the chicken for 6 minutes.
7. Transfer them to a plate and grill the remaining thighs.
8. Serve warm.

Nutritional Information per Serving:

- Calories 388
- Total Fat 8 g
- Saturated Fat 1 g
- Cholesterol 153mg
- sodium 339 mg
- Total Carbs 8 g
- Fiber 1 g
- Sugar 2 g
- Protein 13 g

Grilled Duck Breasts

Preparation Time: 10 minutes
Cooking time: 6 minutes
Serving: 4

Ingredients:

- 1/4 cup olive oil
- 1 tablespoon dried oregano
- 2 pounds duck breasts
- 3 large garlic cloves, grated
- 2 lemons
- Kosher salt and black pepper, to taste

Method:

1. Rub the duck breast with black pepper, salt, lemon juice, garlic, oregano and olive oil.
2. Place the duck breasts in a plate, cover and marinate for 30 minutes.
3. Turn the "Selector" knob to the "Grill Panini" side.
4. Preheat the bottom grill of Cuisine Griddler at 350 degrees F and the upper grill plate on medium heat.
5. Once it is preheated, open the lid and place the duck breasts in the Griddler.
6. Close the griddler's lid and grill the duck for 6 minutes.
7. Serve warm.

Nutritional Information per Serving:

- Calories 301
- Total Fat 15.8 g
- Saturated Fat 2.7 g
- Cholesterol 75 mg
- Sodium 189 mg
- Total Carbs 31.7 g
- Fiber 0.3 g
- Sugar 0.1 g
- Protein 28.2 g

Grilled Chicken Skewers

Preparation Time: 10 minutes
Cooking time: 5 minutes
Serving: 4

Ingredients:

- 1/4 cup fresh lime juice
- 2 garlic cloves, sliced
- 1 chipotle chile in adobo, chopped
- Kosher salt and black pepper, to taste
- 2 boneless chicken breasts, cut into chunks

Method:

1. Mix chicken cubes with black pepper, salt, chile, garlic and lime juice in a bowl.
2. Thread the chicken cubes on the wooden skewers.
3. Turn the "Selector" knob to the "Grill Panini" side.
4. Preheat the bottom grill of Cuisine Griddler at 350 degrees F and the upper grill plate on medium heat.
5. Once it is preheated, open the lid and place the skewers in the Griddler.
6. Close the griddler's lid and grill the skewers for 5 minutes.
7. Serve warm.

Nutritional Information per Serving:

- Calories 440
- Total Fat 7.9 g
- Saturated Fat 1.8 g
- Cholesterol 5 mg
- Sodium 581 mg
- Total Carbs 21.8 g
- Sugar 7.1 g
- Fiber 2.6 g
- Protein 37.2 g

Chicken Burgers

Preparation Time: 10 minutes
Cooking time: 6 minutes
Serving: 5

Ingredients:

- 1 tablespoon butter, melted
- 1 small red onion, chopped
- 2 garlic cloves, chopped
- 2 tablespoons tomato paste
- 1 teaspoon sugar
- 1 tablespoon Worcestershire sauce
- 1 tablespoon hot sauce
- 1 1/4 pounds ground chicken
- 3 tablespoons olive oil
- 2 tablespoons honey

Method:

1. Mix onion, butter, garlic, ground chicken, olive oil, honey, Worcestershire sauce, and sugar in a bowl.
2. Make the chicken patties out of this mixture.
3. Turn the "Selector" knob to the "Grill Panini" side.
4. Preheat the bottom grill of Cuisine Griddler at 350 degrees F and the upper grill plate on medium heat.
5. Once it is preheated, open the lid and place the patties in the Griddler.
6. Close the griddler's lid and grill the patties for 6 minutes.
7. Serve warm.

Nutritional Information per Serving:

- Calories 529
- Total Fat 17 g
- Saturated Fat 3 g
- Cholesterol 65 mg
- Sodium 391 mg
- Total Carbs 55 g
- Fiber 6 g
- Sugar 8 g
- Protein 41g

Tequila Chicken

Preparation Time: 10 minutes
Cooking time: 7 minutes
Serving: 3

Ingredients:

- 1/2 cup gold tequila
- 1 cup lime juice
- 1/2 cup orange juice
- 1 tablespoon chili powder
- 1 tablespoon minced jalapeno pepper
- 1 tablespoon minced fresh garlic
- 2 teaspoons kosher salt
- 1 teaspoon black pepper
- 3 boneless chicken breasts

Method:

1. Mix tequila, lime juice, orange juice, chili powder, jalapeno pepper, garlic, black pepper and salt in a bowl.
2. Add chicken breasts to the tequila marinade, cover and marinate for 1 hour.
3. Turn the "Selector" knob to the "Grill Panini" side.
4. Preheat the bottom grill of Cuisine Griddler at 350 degrees F and the upper grill plate on medium heat.
5. Once it is preheated, open the lid and place the chicken breasts in the Griddler.
6. Close the griddler's lid and grill the chicken breasts for 7 minutes.
7. Serve warm.

Nutritional Information per Serving:

- Calories 352
- Total Fat 14 g
- Saturated Fat 2 g
- Cholesterol 65 mg
- Sodium 220 mg
- Total Carbs 15.8 g
- Fiber 0.2 g
- Sugar 1 g
- Protein 26 g

Grilled Chicken Breast

Preparation Time: 10 minutes
Cooking time: 12 minutes
Serving: 2

Ingredients:

- 3 tablespoons olive oil
- 5 fresh basil leaves, torn
- 1 clove garlic, sliced
- 2 chicken breasts, boneless, skinless
- Kosher salt and black pepper, to taste

Method:

1. Rub the chicken breasts with black pepper, salt, garlic, basil leaves and olive oil.
2. Turn the "Selector" knob to the "Grill Panini" side.
3. Preheat the bottom grill of Cuisine Griddler at 350 degrees F and the upper grill plate on medium heat.
4. Once it is preheated, open the lid and place the chicken breasts in the Griddler.
5. Close the griddler's lid and grill the skewers for 12 minutes.
6. Serve warm.

Nutritional Information per Serving:

- Calories 453
- Total Fat 2.4 g
- Saturated Fat 3 g
- Cholesterol 21 mg
- Sodium 216 mg
- Total Carbs 18 g
- Fiber 2.3 g
- Sugar 1.2 g
- Protein 23.2 g

Grilled Honey Chicken

Preparation Time: 10 minutes
Cooking time: 6 minutes
Serving: 4

Ingredients:

- Juice of 2 lemons
- ½ tablespoon Dijon mustard
- 1 tablespoon honey
- A dash of salt
- 2 whole chicken breasts

Method:

1. Rub the chicken with honey, salt, Dijon and lemon juice.
2. Turn the "Selector" knob to the "Grill Panini" side.
3. Preheat the bottom grill of Cuisine Griddler at 350 degrees F and the upper grill plate on medium heat.
4. Once it is preheated, open the lid and place the chicken breasts in the Griddler.
5. Close the griddler's lid and grill the chicken for 6 minutes.
6. Serve warm.

Nutritional Information per Serving:

- Calories 231
- Total Fat 20.1 g
- Saturated Fat 2.4 g
- Cholesterol 110 mg
- Sodium 941 mg
- Total Carbs 30.1 g
- Fiber 0.9 g
- Sugar 1.4 g
- Protein 14.6 g

Chapter 6: Beef, Pork and Lamb Recipes

Greek Souzoukaklia

Preparation Time: 10 minutes
Cooking time: 14 minutes
Serving: 4

Ingredients:

- 1 ½ pounds ground beef
- 1 onion, chopped
- ⅜ cup raisins, chopped
- 1 ½ teaspoons parsley, chopped
- ½ teaspoon cayenne pepper
- ½ teaspoon ground cinnamon
- ½ teaspoon ground coriander
- 1 pinch ground nutmeg
- ½ teaspoon white sugar
- Salt and black pepper to taste
- 1 tablespoon vegetable oil

Method:

1. Mix ground beef with onion, raisins, and rest of the ingredients in a bowl.
2. Take a handful of this mixture and wrap it around each skewer to make a sausage.
3. Turn the "Selector" knob to the "Grill Panini" side.
4. Preheat the bottom grill of Cuisine Griddler at 350 degrees F and the upper grill plate on medium heat.
5. Once it is preheated, open the lid and place the skewers in the Griddler.
6. Close the griddler's lid and grill the skewers for 15 minutes.
7. Enjoy.

Nutritional Information per Serving:

- Calories 361
- Total Fat 16.3 g
- Saturated Fat 4.9 g
- Cholesterol 114 mg
- Sodium 515 mg
- Total Carbs 19.3 g
- Fiber 0.1 g

- Sugar 18.2 g
- Protein 33.3 g

Margarita Beef Skewers

Preparation Time: 10 minutes
Cooking time: 10 minutes
Serving: 6

Ingredients:

- 1 cup margarita mix
- ½ teaspoon salt
- 1 tablespoon white sugar
- 2 garlic cloves, minced
- ¼ cup vegetable oil
- 1-pound top sirloin steak, cubed
- 16 mushrooms, stems trimmed
- 1 onion, cut into chunks
- 1 large red bell pepper, diced

Method:

1. Mix margarita, salt, white sugar, garlic, vegetable, sirloin steak, mushrooms, onion, and red bell pepper on a bowl.
2. Cover and refrigerate the beef mixture for 1 hour for marination.
3. Thread the beef, mushrooms, onion and bell pepper, alternately on the wooden.
4. Turn the "Selector" knob to the "Grill Panini" side.
5. Preheat the bottom grill of Cuisine Griddler at 350 degrees F and the upper grill plate on medium heat.
6. Once it is preheated, open the lid and place the skewers in the Griddler.
7. Close the griddler's lid and grill the skewers for 10 minutes.
8. Serve warm.

Nutritional Information per Serving:

- Calories 405
- Total Fat 22.7 g
- Saturated Fat 6.1 g
- Cholesterol 4 mg
- Sodium 227 mg
- Total Carbs 26.1 g
- Fiber 1.4 g
- Sugar 0.9 g
- Protein 45.2 g

Cheese Burgers

Preparation Time: 10 minutes
Cooking time: 8 minutes
Serving: 4

Ingredients:

- 1/2 cup cheddar cheese, shredded
- 6 tablespoons chili sauce
- 1 tablespoon chili powder
- 1-lb. ground beef

Method:

1. First, take all the ingredients for patties in a bowl.
2. Thoroughly mix them together then make 4 of the ½ inch patties out of it.
3. Turn the "Selector" knob to the "Grill Panini" side.
4. Preheat the bottom grill of Cuisine Griddler at 350 degrees F and the upper grill plate on medium heat.
5. Once it is preheated, open the lid and place the patties in the Griddler.
6. Close the griddler's lid and grill the patties for 8 minutes.
7. Serve warm.

Nutritional Information per Serving:

- Calories 537
- Total Fat 19.8 g
- Saturated Fat 1.4 g
- Cholesterol 10 mg
- Sodium 719 mg
- Total Carbs 15.1 g
- Fiber 0.9 g
- Sugar 1.4 g
- Protein 37.8 g

Sweet Ham Kabobs

Preparation Time: 10 minutes
Cooking time: 7 minutes
Serving: 6

Ingredients:

- 1 can (20 oz.) pineapple chunks
- 1/2 cup orange marmalade
- 1 tablespoon mustard
- ¼ teaspoon ground cloves
- 1 lb. ham, diced
- ½ lb. Swiss cheese, diced
- 1 medium green pepper, cubed

Method:

1. Take 2 tablespoons of pineapple from pineapples in a bowl.
2. Add mustard, marmalade, and cloves mix well and keep it aside.
3. Thread the pineapple, green pepper, cheese, and ham over the skewers alternatively.
4. Turn the "Selector" knob to the "Grill Panini" side.
5. Preheat the bottom grill of Cuisine Griddler at 350 degrees F and the upper grill plate on medium heat.
6. Once it is preheated, open the lid and place the skewers in the Griddler.
7. Close the griddler's lid and grill the skewers for 7 minutes.
8. Serve warm with marmalade sauce on top.
9. Enjoy.

Nutritional Information per Serving:

- Calories 301
- Total Fat 8.9 g
- Saturated Fat 4.5 g
- Cholesterol 57 mg
- Sodium 340 mg
- Total Carbs 24.7 g
- Fiber 1.2 g
- Sugar 1.3 g
- Protein 15.3 g

Grilled Pork Chops

Preparation Time: 10 minutes
Cooking time: 20 minutes
Serving: 4

Ingredients:

- 4 pork chops bone in
- 1/4 cup olive oil
- 1 1/2 tablespoons brown sugar
- 2 teaspoons Dijon mustard
- 1 1/2 tablespoons soy sauce
- 1 teaspoon lemon zest
- 2 teaspoons parsley chopped
- 2 teaspoons thyme leaves, chopped
- 1/2 teaspoon salt
- 1/2 teaspoon black pepper
- 1 teaspoon garlic, minced

Method:

1. Mix olive oil, brown sugar, Dijon mustard, soy sauce, lemon zest, parsley, thyme, salt, black pepper and garlic in a large and shallow bowl.
2. Add pork chops to the mixture and rub the spices all over.
3. Cover the pork chops and refrigerate for 1-8 hours for marination.
4. Turn the "Selector" knob to the "Grill Panini" side.
5. Preheat the bottom grill of Cuisine Griddler at 350 degrees F and the upper grill plate on medium heat.
6. Once it is preheated, open the lid and place 2 pork chops in the Griddler.
7. Close the griddler's lid and grill the pork chops for 10 minutes.
8. Cook the rest of the chops in the same way.
9. Serve warm.

Nutritional Information per Serving:

- Calories 545
- Total Fat 36.4 g
- Saturated Fat 10.1 g
- Cholesterol 200 mg
- Sodium 272 mg
- Total Carbs 40.7 g

- Fiber 0.2 g
- Sugar 0.1 g
- Protein 42.5 g

Salisbury Steak

Preparation Time: 10 minutes
Cooking time: 12 minutes
Serving: 5

Ingredients:

- 1 1/2 pounds lean ground beef
- 1/2 cup seasoned breadcrumbs
- 1 tablespoon ketchup
- 2 teaspoons dry mustard
- 4 dashes Worcestershire sauce
- 1 cube beef bouillon, crumbled
- Salt and black pepper, to taste
- 1 tablespoon butter, melted

Method:

1. Mix ground beef with breadcrumbs, ketchup, mustard, Worcestershire sauce, beef bouillon, butter, black pepper and salt in a bowl.
2. Make five patties out of the crumbly beef mixture.
3. Turn the "Selector" knob to the "Grill Panini" side.
4. Preheat the bottom grill of Cuisine Griddler at 350 degrees F and the upper grill plate on medium heat.
5. Once it is preheated, open the lid and place the patties in the Griddler.
6. Close the griddler's lid and grill the patties for 6 minutes.
7. Serve warm.

Nutritional Information per Serving:

- Calories 548
- Total Fat 22.9 g
- Saturated Fat 9 g
- Cholesterol 105 mg
- Sodium 350 mg
- Total Carbs 17.5 g
- Sugar 10.9 g
- Fiber 6.3 g
- Protein 40.1 g

Teriyaki Beef Skewers

Preparation Time: 10 minutes
Cooking time: 6 minutes
Serving: 6

Ingredients:

- ¾ cup brown sugar
- ¼ cup soy sauce
- 1/8 cup pineapple juice
- 1/8 cup water
- 2 tablespoons vegetable oil
- 1 garlic clove, chopped
- 2 pounds boneless round steak, sliced

Method:

1. Mix brown sugar, soy sauce, pineapple juice, water, vegetable oi, garlic cloves and steak slices in a bowl.
2. Cover and refrigerate the steaks for 24 hours for marination.
3. Thread the marinated beef on the wooden skewers.
4. Turn the "Selector" knob to the "Grill Panini" side.
5. Preheat the bottom grill of Cuisine Griddler at 350 degrees F and the upper grill plate on medium heat.
6. Once it is preheated, open the lid and place the skewers in the Griddler.
7. Close the griddler's lid and grill the skewers for 6 minutes.
8. Serve warm.

Nutritional Information per Serving:

- Calories 380
- Total Fat 20 g
- Saturated Fat 5 g
- Cholesterol 151 mg
- Sodium 686 mg
- Total Carbs 33 g
- Fiber 1 g
- Sugar 1.2 g
- Protein 21 g

Chimichurri Beef Skewers

Preparation Time: 10 minutes
Cooking time: 8 minutes
Serving: 6

Ingredients:

- 1/3 cup fresh basil
- 1/3 cup fresh cilantro
- 1/3 cup fresh parsley
- 1 tablespoon red wine vinegar
- Juice of 1/2 lemon
- 1 garlic clove, minced
- 1 shallot, minced
- 1/2 teaspoon crushed red pepper flakes
- 1/2 cup olive oil, divided
- Salt to taste
- Black pepper to taste
- 1 red onion, cubed
- 1 red pepper, cubed
- 1 orange pepper, cubed
- 1 yellow pepper, cubed
- 1 1/2 lb. sirloin steak, fat trimmed and diced

Method:

1. First, take basil, parsley, vinegar, lemon juice, red pepper, shallots, garlic, and cilantro in a blender jug.
2. Blend well, then add ¼ cup olive oil, salt, and pepper and mix again.
3. Now thread the steak, bell peppers, and onion, alternately on the skewers.
4. Drizzle salt, black pepper, and remaining oil over the skewers.
5. Turn the "Selector" knob to the "Grill Panini" side.
6. Preheat the bottom grill of Cuisine Griddler at 350 degrees F and the upper grill plate on medium heat.
7. Once it is preheated, open the lid and place the skewers in the Griddler.
8. Close the griddler's lid and grill the skewers for 8 minutes.
9. Serve warm with green sauce.

Nutritional Information per Serving:

- Calories 231

- Total Fat 20.1 g
- Saturated Fat 2.4 g
- Cholesterol 110 mg
- Sodium 941 mg
- Total Carbs 20.1 g
- Fiber 0.9 g
- Sugar 1.4 g
- Protein 14.6 g

Flank Steak

Preparation Time: 10 minutes
Cooking time: 10 minutes
Serving: 4

Ingredients:

- 1/2 cup 1 tablespoon soy sauce
- 1/4 cup 2 tablespoon vegetable oil
- 1/2 cup rice wine vinegar
- 4 garlic cloves, minced
- 2 tablespoon ginger, minced
- 2 tablespoon honey
- 3 tablespoon sesame oil
- 3 tablespoon Sriracha
- 1 1/2 lb. flank steak
- 1 teaspoon sugar
- 1 teaspoon red pepper flakes
- 2 large cucumbers, sliced
- Salt to taste

Method:

1. Mix ½ cup soy sauce, half of the rice wine, honey, ginger, garlic, 2 tablespoon Sriracha sauce, 2 tablespoon sesame oil, and vegetable oil in a large bowl.
2. Pour half of this sauce over the steak and rub it well.
3. Cover the steak and marinate for 10 minutes.
4. For salad mix cucumber with remaining rice wine vinegar, sesame oil, sugar, red pepper flakes, Sriracha sauce, soy sauce, and salt in a salad bowl.
5. Turn the "Selector" knob to the "Grill Panini" side.
6. Preheat the bottom grill of Cuisine Griddler at 350 degrees F and the upper grill plate on medium heat.
7. Once it is preheated, open the lid and place the steak in the Griddler.
8. Close the griddler's lid and grill the flank steaks for 10 minutes until done.
9. Serve warm with cucumber salad.

Nutritional Information per Serving:

- Calories 327
- Total Fat 3.5 g
- Saturated Fat 0.5 g

- Cholesterol 162 mg
- Sodium 142 mg
- Total Carbs 33.6 g
- Fiber 0.4 g
- Sugar 0.5 g
- Protein 24.5 g

Grilled Lamb with Herbes De Provence

Preparation Time: 10 minutes
Cooking time: 18 minutes
Serving: 6

Ingredients:

- 1 rib (3 ounces-1-inch-thick) lamb chops
- 1/4 cups olive oil
- 2 lemons, juiced
- Salt and black pepper, to taste
- 3 tablespoons Herbes de Provence

Method:

1. Rub the lamb chops with lemon juice, olive oil, black pepper, salt and Herbes de Provence.
2. Cover and marinate the chops for 1 hour in the refrigerator.
3. Turn the "Selector" knob to the "Grill Panini" side.
4. Preheat the bottom grill of Cuisine Griddler at 350 degrees F and the upper grill plate on medium heat.
5. Once it is preheated, open the lid and place half of the chops in the Griddler.
6. Close the griddler's lid and grill the chops for 9 minutes.
7. Transfer the grilled chops to a plate and grill the remaining chops in the same manner.
8. Serve warm.

Nutritional Information per Serving:

- Calories 308
- Total Fat 20.5 g
- Saturated Fat 3 g
- Cholesterol 42 mg
- Sodium 688 mg
- Total Carbs 40.3 g
- Sugar 1.4 g
- Fiber 4.3 g
- Protein 49 g

Raspberry Pork Chops

Preparation Time: 10 minutes
Cooking time: 20 minutes
Serving: 4

Ingredients:

- 1/2 cup raspberry preserves
- 1 chipotle in adobo sauce, chopped
- 1/2 teaspoon salt
- 4 bone-in pork loin chops

Method:

1. Take a small pan and mix preserves with chipotle pepper sauce on medium heat.
2. Keep ¼ cup of this sauce aside and rub the remaining over the pork.
3. Sprinkle salt over the pork and mix well.
4. Turn the "Selector" knob to the "Grill Panini" side.
5. Preheat the bottom grill of Cuisine Griddler at 350 degrees F and the upper grill plate on medium heat.
6. Once it is preheated, open the lid and place 2 pork chops in the Griddler.
7. Close the griddler's lid and grill the chops for 10 minutes.
8. Transfer them to a serving plate and grill remaining chops in the same manner.
9. Pour the reserved sauce over the pork chops.
10. Serve warm.

Nutritional Information per Serving:

- Calories 401
- Total Fat 50.5 g
- Saturated Fat 11.7 g
- Cholesterol 58 mg
- Sodium 463 mg
- Total Carbs 9.9 g
- Fiber 1.5 g
- Sugar 0.3 g
- Protein 29.3 g

American Burger

Preparation Time: 10 minutes
Cooking time: 9 minutes
Serving: 4

Ingredients:

- 1/2 cup seasoned bread crumbs
- 1 large egg, lightly beaten
- 1/2 teaspoon salt
- 1/2 teaspoon pepper
- 1-lb. ground beef
- 1 tablespoon olive oil

Method:

1. Take all the ingredients for a burger in a suitable bowl except the oil and the buns.
2. Mix them thoroughly together and make 4 of the ½ inch patties.
3. Brush these patties with olive oil.
4. Turn the "Selector" knob to the "Grill Panini" side.
5. Preheat the bottom grill of Cuisine Griddler at 350 degrees F and the upper grill plate on medium heat.
6. Once it is preheated, open the lid and place the patties in the Griddler.
7. Close the griddler's lid and grill the patties for 7-9 minutes.
8. Serve warm.

Nutritional Information per Serving:

- Calories 301
- Total Fat 15.8 g
- Saturated Fat 2.7 g
- Cholesterol 75 mg
- Sodium 389 mg
- Total Carbs 11.7 g
- Fiber 0.3g
- Sugar 0.1 g
- Protein 28.2 g

Fajita Skewers

Preparation Time: 10 minutes
Cooking time: 7 minutes
Serving: 6

Ingredients:

- 1 lb. sirloin steak, cubed
- 1 bunch scallions, cut into large pieces
- 1 pack flour tortillas, cut into triangles
- 4 large bell peppers, cubed
- olive oil, for drizzling
- Salt to taste
- Black pepper to taste

Method:

1. Thread the steak, tortillas, peppers, and scallions on the skewers.
2. Drizzle salt, black pepper, and olive oil over the skewers.
3. Turn the "Selector" knob to the "Grill Panini" side.
4. Preheat the bottom grill of Cuisine Griddler at 350 degrees F and the upper grill plate on medium heat.
5. Once it is preheated, open the lid and place the fajita skewers in the Griddler.
6. Close the griddler's lid and grill the skewers for 7 minutes.
7. Serve warm.

Nutritional Information per Serving:

- Calories 353
- Total Fat 7.5 g
- Saturated Fat 1.1 g
- Cholesterol 20 mg
- Sodium 297 mg
- Total Carbs 10.4 g
- Fiber 0.2 g
- Sugar 0.1 g
- Protein 13.1 g

Honey Glazed Pork Chops

Preparation Time: 10 minutes
Cooking time: 20 minutes
Serving: 4

Ingredients:

- 1/4 cup honey
- 1/2 cup low-sodium soy sauce
- 2 garlic cloves, minced
- Red pepper flakes, to taste
- 4 boneless pork chops

Method:

1. Mix honey, soy sauce, garlic and red pepper flakes in a bowl.
2. Brush this honey mixture over the pork chops, liberally then marinate for 30 minutes.
3. Turn the "Selector" knob to the "Grill Panini" side.
4. Preheat the bottom grill of Cuisine Griddler at 350 degrees F and the upper grill plate on medium heat.
5. Once it is preheated, open the lid and place 2 pork chops in the Griddler.
6. Close the griddler's lid and grill the chops for 10 minutes.
7. Transfer these chops to a plate and grill the remaining chops in the same manner.
8. Serve warm.

Nutritional Information per Serving:

- Calories 695
- Total Fat 17.5 g
- Saturated Fat 4.8 g
- Cholesterol 283 mg
- Sodium 355 mg
- Total Carbs 26.4 g
- Fiber 1.8 g
- Sugar 0.8 g
- Protein 47.4 g

Grilled Lamb Chops

Preparation Time: 10 minutes
Cooking time: 18 minutes
Serving: 6

Ingredients:

- 2 large garlic cloves, crushed
- 1 tablespoon fresh rosemary leaves
- 1 teaspoon fresh thyme leaves
- Pinch cayenne pepper, to taste
- Sea salt, to taste
- 2 tablespoons olive oil
- 6 lamb chops, about 3/4-inch thick

Method:

1. Rub the lamb chops with olive oil, garlic, rosemary, thyme, salt and cayenne pepper.
2. Cover the chops and marinate for 1-8 hours in the refrigerator.
3. Turn the "Selector" knob to the "Grill Panini" side.
4. Preheat the bottom grill of Cuisine Griddler at 350 degrees F and the upper grill plate on medium heat.
5. Once it is preheated, open the lid and place 3 chops in the Griddler.
6. Close the griddler's lid and grill the chops for 9 minutes.
7. Transfer them to a plate and grill the remaining chops in the same manner.
8. Serve warm.

Nutritional Information per Serving:

- Calories 452
- Total Fat 4 g
- Saturated Fat 2 g
- Cholesterol 65 mg
- Sodium 220 mg
- Total Carbs 23.1 g
- Fiber 0.3 g
- Sugar 1 g
- Protein 26g

Lamb Skewers

Preparation Time: 10 minutes
Cooking time: 10 minutes
Serving: 6

Ingredients:

- 1 (10 oz.) pack couscous
- 1 1/2 cup yogurt
- 1 tablespoon 1 teaspoon cumin
- 2 garlic cloves, minced
- Juice of 2 lemons
- Salt to taste
- Black pepper to taste
- 1 1/2 lb. leg of lamb, boneless, diced
- 2 tomatoes, diced
- 1/2 English cucumber, diced
- 1/2 small red onion, chopped
- 1/4 cup parsley, chopped
- 1/4 cup fresh mint, chopped
- 3 tablespoon olive oil

Method:

1. First, cook the couscous as per the given instructions on the package then fluff with a fork.
2. Whisk yogurt with garlic, cumin, lemon juice, salt, and black pepper in a large bowl.
3. Add lamb and mix well to coat the meat.
4. Separately toss red onion with cucumber, tomatoes, parsley, mint, lemon juice, olive oil, salt, and couscous in salad bowl.
5. Thread the seasoned lamb on 8 skewers and drizzle salt and black pepper over them.
6. Turn the "Selector" knob to the "Grill Panini" side.
7. Preheat the bottom grill of Cuisine Griddler at 350 degrees F and the upper grill plate on medium heat.
8. Once it is preheated, open the lid and place the lamb skewers in the Griddler.
9. Close the griddler's lid and grill the lamb skewers for 10 minutes.
10. Serve warm with prepared couscous.

Nutritional Information per Serving:

- Calories 472
- Total Fat 11.1 g
- Saturated Fat 5.8 g
- Cholesterol 610 mg
- Sodium 749 mg
- Total Carbs 19.9 g
- Fiber 0.2 g
- Sugar 0.2 g
- Protein 13.5 g

Chapter 7: Seafood Recipes

Pistachio Pesto Shrimp

Preparation Time: 10 minutes
Cooking time: 4 minutes
Serving: 4

Ingredients:

- ¾ cup fresh arugula
- ½ cup fresh parsley, minced
- 1/3 cup shelled pistachios
- 2 tablespoons lemon juice
- 1 garlic clove, peeled
- ¼ teaspoon lemon zest, grated
- ½ cup olive oil
- ¼ cup Parmesan cheese, shredded
- ¼ teaspoon salt
- 1/8 teaspoon pepper
- 1 ½ lbs. jumbo shrimp, peeled and deveined

Method:

1. Start by blending the arugula, parsley, pistachios, lemon juice, garlic, lemon zest, and olive oil in a blender until smooth.
2. Stir in salt, black pepper, Parmesan cheese, and mix well.
3. Toss the shrimp with the prepared sauce in a bowl then cover to refrigerate for 30 minutes.
4. Thread these pesto shrimps on the wooden skewers.
5. Turn the "Selector" knob to the "Grill Panini" side.
6. Preheat the bottom grill of Cuisine Griddler at 350 degrees F and the upper grill plate on medium heat.
7. Once it is preheated, open the lid and place the pesto skewers in the Griddler.
8. Close the griddler's lid and grill the shrimp skewers for 4 minutes.
9. Serve warm.

Nutritional Information per Serving:

- Calories 293
- Total Fat 16 g
- Saturated Fat 2.3 g

- Cholesterol 75 mg
- Sodium 386 mg
- Total Carbs 5.2 g
- Sugar 2.6 g
- Fiber 1.9 g
- Protein 34.2 g

Grilled Garlic Scallops

Preparation Time: 10 minutes
Cooking time: 4 minutes
Serving: 4

Ingredients:

- 1/4 cup olive oil
- Juice of 1 lemon
- 3 garlic cloves minced
- 1 tablespoon Italian seasoning
- Salt and black pepper, to taste
- 1-pound scallops

Method:

1. Mix Italian seasoning, black pepper, salt, garlic cloves, lemon juice and olive oil in a bowl.
2. Toss in scallops, mix gently, cover and refrigerate for 30 minutes.
3. Turn the "Selector" knob to the "Griddle" side.
4. Preheat the bottom grill of Cuisine Griddler at 350 degrees F.
5. Once it is preheated, open the lid and place the scallops in the Griddler.
6. Grill the scallop for 2 minutes flip and grill for 2 minutes.
7. Serve warm.

Nutritional Information per Serving:

- Calories 351
- Total Fat 4 g
- Saturated Fat 6.3 g
- Cholesterol 360 mg
- Sodium 236 mg
- Total Carbs 19.1 g
- Sugar 0.3 g
- Fiber 0.1 g
- Protein 36 g

Blackened Salmon

Preparation Time: 10 minutes
Cooking time: 6 minutes
Serving: 2

Ingredients:

- 1 lb. salmon fillets
- 3 tablespoons butter, melted
- 1 tablespoon lemon pepper
- 1 teaspoon seasoned salt
- 1½ tablespoon smoked paprika
- 1 teaspoon cayenne pepper
- ¾ teaspoon onion salt
- ½ teaspoon dry basil
- ½ teaspoon ground white pepper
- ½ teaspoon ground black pepper
- ¼ teaspoon dry oregano
- ¼ teaspoon ancho chili powder

Method:

1. Liberally season the salmon fillets with butter and other ingredients.
2. Turn the "Selector" knob to the "Grill Panini" side.
3. Preheat the bottom grill of Cuisine Griddler at 350 degrees F and the upper grill plate on medium heat.
4. Once it is preheated, open the lid and place the salmon fillets in the Griddler.
5. Close the griddler's lid and grill the fish fillets for 6 minutes.
6. Serve warm.

Nutritional Information per Serving:

- Calories 378
- Total Fat 7 g
- Saturated Fat 8.1 g
- Cholesterol 230 mg
- Sodium 316 mg
- Total Carbs 16.2 g
- Sugar 0.2 g
- Fiber 0.3 g
- Protein 26 g

Lemon-Garlic Salmon

Preparation Time: 10 minutes
Cooking time: 7 minutes
Serving: 4

Ingredients:

- 2 garlic cloves, minced
- 2 teaspoons lemon zest, grated
- 1/2 teaspoon salt
- 1/2 teaspoon fresh rosemary, minced
- 1/2 teaspoon black pepper
- 4 salmon fillets (6 oz.)

Method:

1. Mix garlic with lemon zest, salt, rosemary and black pepper in a bowl
2. Leave this spice mixture for 15 minutes then rub it over the salmon with this mixture.
3. Turn the "Selector" knob to the "Grill Panini" side.
4. Preheat the bottom grill of Cuisine Griddler at 350 degrees F and the upper grill plate on medium heat.
5. Once it is preheated, open the lid and place the salmon in the Griddler.
6. Close the griddler's lid and grill the salmon for 7 minutes.
7. Serve warm.

Nutritional Information per Serving:

- Calories 246
- Total Fat 7.4 g
- Saturated Fat 4.6 g
- Cholesterol 105 mg
- Sodium 353 mg
- Total Carbs 19.4 g
- Sugar 6.5 g
- Fiber 2.7 g
- Protein 37.2 g

Shrimp Skewers

Preparation Time: 10 minutes
Cooking time: 4 minutes
Serving: 4

Ingredients:

- 1/3 cup lemon juice
- 2 tablespoons olive oil
- 2 garlic cloves, minced
- 1/2 teaspoon lemon zest, grated
- 1 lb. uncooked shrimp, peeled and deveined
- Salt and black pepper, to taste

Method:

1. Season the shrimp with olive oil, salt, black pepper lemon juice, lemon zest, oil, and garlic in a suitable bowl.
2. Thread the seasoned shrimp on the skewers.
3. And season the skewers with salt and black pepper.
4. Turn the "Selector" knob to the "Grill Panini" side.
5. Preheat the bottom grill of Cuisine Griddler at 350 degrees F and the upper grill plate on medium heat.
6. Once it is preheated, open the lid and place the shrimp skewers in the Griddler.
7. Close the griddler's lid and grill the skewers for 4 minutes.
8. Serve warm.

Nutritional Information per Serving:

- Calories 338
- Total Fat 3.8 g
- Saturated Fat 0.7 g
- Cholesterol 22 mg
- Sodium 620 mg
- Total Carbs 28.3 g
- Fiber 2.4 g
- Sugar 1.2 g
- Protein 15.4 g

Ginger Salmon

Preparation Time: 10 minutes
Cooking time: 8 minutes
Serving: 3

Ingredients:

Sauce:

- ¼ tablespoons rice vinegar
- 1 teaspoons sugar
- 1/8 teaspoon salt
- ¼ tablespoon lime zest, grated
- 1/8 cup lime juice
- ½ tablespoon olive oil
- 1/8 teaspoon ground coriander
- 1/8 teaspoon ground black pepper
- 1/8 cup cilantro, chopped
- ¼ tablespoon onion, chopped
- ½ teaspoon ginger root, minced
- 1 garlic clove, minced
- 1 small cucumber, peeled, chopped

Salmon:

- 2 tablespoons gingerroot, minced
- ¼ tablespoon lime juice
- ¼ tablespoon olive oil
- Salt, to taste
- Black pepper, to taste
- 3 (6 oz.) salmon fillets

Method:

1. Start by blending the cucumber with all the sauce ingredients in a blender until smooth.
2. Season and rub the salmon fillets with ginger, oil, salt, black pepper, lime juice.
3. Turn the "Selector" knob to the "Grill Panini" side.
4. Preheat the bottom grill of Cuisine Griddler at 350 degrees F and the upper grill plate on medium heat.
5. Once it is preheated, open the lid and place the salmon fillets in the Griddler.
6. Close the griddler's lid and grill the salmon fillets for 8 minutes.

7. Serve warm with cucumber sauce.

Nutritional Information per Serving:

- Calories 457
- Total Fat 19.1 g
- Saturated Fat 11 g
- Cholesterol 262 mg
- Sodium 557 mg
- Total Carbs 18.9 g
- Sugar 1.2 g
- Fiber 1.7 g
- Protein 32.5 g

Barbecue Squid

Preparation Time: 10 minutes
Cooking time: 3 minutes
Serving: 4

Ingredients:

- 1 ½ pounds skinless squid tubes, sliced
- ⅓ cup red bell pepper, chopped
- 13 fresh red Thai chiles, stemmed
- 6 garlic cloves, minced
- 3 shallots, chopped
- 1 (1-inch) piece fresh ginger, chopped
- 6 tablespoons sugar
- 2 tablespoons soy sauce
- 1 ½ teaspoons black pepper
- ¼ teaspoon salt

Method:

1. Blend bell pepper, red chilies, shallots, sugar, soy sauce, black pepper and salt in a blender.
2. Transfer this marinade to a Ziplock bag and ad squid tubes.
3. Seal the bag and refrigerate for 1 hour for marination.
4. Turn the "Selector" knob to the "Grill Panini" side.
5. Preheat the bottom grill of Cuisine Griddler at 350 degrees F and the upper grill plate on medium heat.
6. Once it is preheated, open the lid and place the squid chunks in the Griddler.
7. Close the griddler's lid and grill the squid for 2-3 minutes.
8. Serve warm.

Nutritional Information per Serving:

- Calories 248
- Total Fat 15.7 g
- Saturated Fat 2.7 g
- Cholesterol 75 mg
- Sodium 94 mg
- Total Carbs 31.4 g
- Fiber 0.4 g
- Sugar 3.1 g

- Protein 24.9 g

Salmon Lime Burgers

Preparation Time: 10 minutes
Cooking time: 6 minutes
Serving: 2

Ingredients:

- 1-lb. skinless salmon fillets, minced
- 2 tablespoons grated lime zest
- 1 tablespoon Dijon mustard
- 3 tablespoons shallot, chopped
- 2 tablespoons fresh cilantro, minced
- 1 tablespoon soy sauce
- 1 tablespoon honey
- 3 garlic cloves, minced
- 1/2 teaspoon salt
- 1/4 teaspoon black pepper

Method:

1. Thoroughly mix all the ingredients for burgers in a bowl.
2. Make four patties out this salmon mixture.
3. Turn the "Selector" knob to the "Grill Panini" side.
4. Preheat the bottom grill of Cuisine Griddler at 350 degrees F and the upper grill plate on medium heat.
5. Once it is preheated, open the lid and place the salmon burgers in the Griddler.
6. Close the griddler's lid and grill the salmon burgers for 6 minutes.
7. Serve warm with buns.

Nutritional Information per Serving:

- Calories 408
- Total Fat 21 g
- Saturated Fat 4.3 g
- Cholesterol 150 mg
- Sodium 146 mg
- Total Carbs 21.1 g
- Sugar 0.1 g
- Fiber 0.4 g
- Protein 23 g

Chapter 8: Vegetable Recipes

Cauliflower Zucchini Skewers

Preparation Time: 10 minutes
Cooking time: 10 minutes
Serving: 8

Ingredients:

- 4 large zucchinis sliced
- 1 head cauliflower, cut into florets
- Olive oil, for drizzling
- kosher salt, to taste
- Black pepper, to taste
- 1/4 cup crumbled feta

Method:

1. Alternately, thread the cauliflower and zucchini slices on the wooden skewers.
2. Drizzle olive oil, black pepper and salt over the skewers.
3. Turn the "Selector" knob to the "Grill Panini" side.
4. Preheat the bottom grill of Cuisine Griddler at 300 degrees F and the upper grill plate on medium heat.
5. Once it is preheated, open the lid and place the skewers in the Griddler.
6. Close the griddler's lid and grill the cauliflower skewers for 10 minutes.
7. Garnish with feta cheese.
8. Serve.

Nutritional Information per Serving:

- Calories 191
- Total Fat 12.2 g
- Saturated Fat 2.4 g
- Cholesterol 110 mg
- Sodium 276 mg
- Total Carbs 5 g
- Fiber 0.9 g
- Sugar 1.4 g
- Protein 8.8 g

Tarragon Asparagus

Preparation Time: 10 minutes
Cooking time: 4 minutes
Serving: 4

Ingredients:

- 2 lbs. fresh asparagus, trimmed
- 2 tablespoons olive oil
- 1 teaspoon salt
- 1/2 teaspoon black pepper
- 1/4 cup honey
- 4 tablespoons fresh tarragon, minced

Method:

1. Liberally season the asparagus by tossing with oil, salt, pepper, honey, and tarragon.
2. Turn the "Selector" knob to the "Grill Panini" side.
3. Preheat the bottom grill of Cuisine Griddler at 300 degrees F and the upper grill plate on medium heat.
4. Once it is preheated, open the lid and place the asparagus in the Griddler.
5. Close the griddler's lid and grill the asparagus for 4 minutes.
6. Serve warm.

Nutritional Information per Serving:

- Calories 148
- Total Fat 15.7 g
- Saturated Fat 2.7 g
- Cholesterol 75 mg
- Sodium 94 mg
- Total Carbs 3.4 g
- Fiber 0.6 g
- Sugar 15 g
- Protein 14.1 g

Butter Glazed Green Beans

Preparation Time: 10 minutes
Cooking time: 5 minutes
Serving: 4

Ingredients:

- 1-lb. fresh green beans, trimmed
- 1/2 teaspoon Cajun seasoning
- 1 tablespoon butter, melted

Method:

1. Toss green beans with butter and Cajun seasoning in a bowl.
2. Turn the "Selector" knob to the "Grill Panini" side.
3. Preheat the bottom grill of Cuisine Griddler at 350 degrees F and the upper grill plate on medium heat.
4. Once it is preheated, open the lid and place the green beans in the Griddler.
5. Close the griddler's lid and grill the green beans for 5 minutes.
6. Serve warm.

Nutritional Information per Serving:

- Calories 304
- Total Fat 30.6 g
- Saturated Fat 13.1 g
- Cholesterol 131 mg
- Sodium 834 mg
- Total Carbs 21.4 g
- Fiber 0.2 g
- Sugar 0.3 g
- Protein 4.6 g

Cauliflower Steaks

Preparation Time: 10 minutes
Cooking time: 9 minutes
Serving: 4

Ingredients:

- 2 large heads cauliflower
- ¼ cup olive oil
- ½ teaspoons garlic powder
- ½ teaspoons paprika
- Kosher salt, to taste
- Black pepper, to taste
- 2 cups cheddar cheese, shredded
- Ranch dressing, for drizzling
- 8 cooked bacon slices, crumbled
- 2 tablespoons chives, chopped

Method:

1. Mix olive oil, garlic powder, paprika, salt, and black pepper in a bowl
2. Slice the cauliflower into ¾ inch thick steaks and rub them with the olive oil mixture.
3. Turn the "Selector" knob to the "Grill Panini" side.
4. Preheat the bottom grill of Cuisine Griddler at 350 degrees F and the upper grill plate on medium heat.
5. Once it is preheated, open the lid and place the cauliflower steaks in the Griddler.
6. Close the griddler's lid and grill the steaks for 8 minutes until lightly charred.
7. Open the lid and drizzle bacon, cheddar cheese, ranch dressing and chives on top.
8. Cook for 1 minute until the cheese is melted.
9. Serve warm.

Nutritional Information per Serving:

- Calories 278
- Total Fat 3.8 g
- Saturated Fat 0.7 g
- Cholesterol 2 mg
- Sodium 620 mg
- Total Carbs 13.3 g
- Fiber 2.4 g

- Sugar 1.2 g
- Protein 5.4 g

Grilled Veggies with Vinaigrette

Preparation Time: 10 minutes
Cooking time: 7 minutes
Serving: 4

Ingredients:

Vinaigrette:

- 1/4 cup red wine vinegar
- 1 tablespoon Dijon mustard
- 1 tablespoon honey
- 1/2 teaspoon salt
- 1/8 teaspoon pepper
- 1/4 cup canola oil
- 1/4 cup olive oil

Vegetables:

- 2 large sweet onions, sliced
- 2 yellow summer squash, sliced
- 2 large red peppers, seeded and sliced

Method:

1. Whisk wine vinegar, Dijon mustard, honey, salt, black pepper olive oil and canola oil in a bowl.
2. Turn the "Selector" knob to the "Grill Panini" side.
3. Preheat the bottom grill of Cuisine Griddler at 350 degrees F and the upper grill plate on medium heat.
4. Once it is preheated, open the lid and place the vegetable slices in the Griddler.
5. Close the griddler's lid and grill the onions and peppers for 5 minutes and summer squash for 7 minutes.
6. Transfer the veggies to a serving plate and drizzle the vinaigrette on top.
7. Serve warm.

Nutritional Information per Serving:

- Calories 341
- Total Fat 4 g
- Saturated Fat 0.5 g
- Cholesterol 69 mg
- Sodium 547 mg

- Total Carbs 6.4 g
- Fiber 1.2 g
- Sugar 1 g
- Protein 10.3 g

Grilled Veggies

Preparation Time: 10 minutes
Cooking time: 8 minutes
Serving: 2

Ingredients:

- 1 eggplant, sliced
- 1 zucchini, sliced
- 1 onion, sliced
- 2 tablespoons olive oil
- 1 tablespoon kosher salt
- 1 tablespoon black pepper

Method:

1. Toss and season all the vegetable slices with oil, black pepper and salt.
2. Turn the "Selector" knob to the "Grill Panini" side.
3. Preheat the bottom grill of Cuisine Griddler at 350 degrees F and the upper grill plate on medium heat.
4. Once it is preheated, open the lid and place the vegetables in the Griddler.
5. Close the griddler's lid and grill the veggies for 8 minutes until lightly charred.
6. Serve warm.

Nutritional Information per Serving:

- Calories 246
- Total Fat 14.8 g
- Saturated Fat 0.7 g
- Cholesterol 22 mg
- Sodium 220 mg
- Total Carbs 10.3 g
- Fiber 2.4 g
- Sugar 1.2 g
- Protein 12.4 g

Grilled Mushroom Skewers

Preparation Time: 10 minutes
Cooking time: 3 minutes
Serving: 6

Ingredients:

- 2 pounds mushrooms, sliced
- 2 tablespoons balsamic vinegar
- 1 tablespoon soy sauce
- 3 garlic cloves, chopped
- 1/2 teaspoon thyme, chopped
- Salt and black pepper to taste

Method:

1. Toss mushrooms with balsamic vinegar, soy sauce, garlic, thyme, black pepper and salt in a bowl.
2. Thread the mushroom slices on mini wooden skewers.
3. Turn the "Selector" knob to the "Grill Panini" side.
4. Preheat the bottom grill of Cuisine Griddler at 350 degrees F and the upper grill plate on medium heat.
5. Once it is preheated, open the lid and place mushroom skewers horizontally in the Griddler.
6. Close the griddler's lid and grill the mushrooms for 3 minutes.
7. Serve warm.

Nutritional Information per Serving:

- Calories 418
- Total Fat 15.7 g
- Saturated Fat 2.7 g
- Cholesterol 75 mg
- Sodium 94 mg
- Total Carbs 10.4 g
- Fiber 0.1 g
- Sugar 0.3 g
- Protein 4.9 g

Grilled Butternut Squash

Preparation Time: 10 minutes
Cooking time: 8 minutes
Serving: 4

Ingredients:

- 1 medium butternut squash, sliced
- 1 tablespoon olive oil
- 1 ½ teaspoons dried oregano
- 1 teaspoon dried thyme
- 1/2 teaspoon salt
- 1/4 teaspoon black pepper

Method:

1. Peel and slice the squash into ½ inch thick slices.
2. Remove the center of the slices to discard the seeds.
3. Toss the squash slices with remaining ingredients in a bowl.
4. Turn the "Selector" knob to the "Grill Panini" side.
5. Preheat the bottom grill of Cuisine Griddler at 350 degrees F and the upper grill plate on medium heat.
6. Once it is preheated, open the lid and place the squash in the Griddler.
7. Close the griddler's lid and grill the squash for 8 minutes.
8. Serve warm.

Nutritional Information per Serving:

- Calories 249
- Total Fat 11.9 g
- Saturated Fat 1.7 g
- Cholesterol 78 mg
- Sodium 79 mg
- Total Carbs 41.8 g
- Fiber 1.1 g
- Sugar 20.3 g
- Protein 15 g

Grilled Brussels Sprouts

Preparation Time: 10 minutes
Cooking time: 9 minutes
Serving: 2

Ingredients:

- 1 lb. brussels sprouts, halved
- 3 tablespoons olive oil
- ¼ cup balsamic vinegar
- 1 tablespoon honey
- 1 tablespoon mustard
- 2 teaspoons crushed red pepper flakes
- Kosher salt
- ½ cup Parmesan, grated

Method:

1. Mix oil, vinegar, honey, mustard, red pepper flakes, and salt in a bowl.
2. Toss in brussels sprout and toss well to coat.
3. Turn the "Selector" knob to the "Grill Panini" side.
4. Preheat the bottom grill of Cuisine Griddler at 350 degrees F and the upper grill plate on medium heat.
5. Once it is preheated, open the lid and place the brussels sprouts in the Griddler.
6. Close the griddler's lid and grill the brussels sprouts for 7-9 minutes until lightly charred.
7. Garnish with parmesan.

Nutritional Information per Serving:

- Calories 121
- Total Fat 3.8 g
- Saturated Fat 0.7 g
- Cholesterol 22 mg
- Sodium 620 mg
- Total Carbs 8.3 g
- Fiber 2.4 g
- Sugar 1.2 g
- Protein 5.4 g

Grilled Eggplant

Preparation Time: 10 minutes
Cooking time: 8 minutes
Serving: 4

Ingredients:

- 2 small eggplants, half-inch slices
- 1/4 cup olive oil
- 2 tablespoons lime juice
- 3 teaspoons Cajun seasoning

Method:

1. Liberally season the eggplant slices with oil, lemon juice, and Cajun seasoning.
2. Turn the "Selector" knob to the "Grill Panini" side.
3. Preheat the bottom grill of Cuisine Griddler at 300 degrees F and the upper grill plate on medium heat.
4. Once it is preheated, open the lid and place the eggplant slices in the Griddler.
5. Close the griddler's lid and grill the eggplant for 8 minutes until slightly charred.
6. Serve warm.

Nutritional Information per Serving:

- Calories 172
- Total Fat 11.1 g
- Saturated Fat 5.8 g
- Cholesterol 610 mg
- Sodium 749 mg
- Total Carbs 16.9 g
- Fiber 0.2 g
- Sugar 0.2 g
- Protein 3.5 g

Grilled Zucchini

Preparation Time: 10 minutes
Cooking time: 5 minutes
Serving: 4

Ingredients:

- 2 medium zucchinis, sliced
- 1 tablespoon olive oil
- 1/2 teaspoons lemon zest
- 1/4 teaspoons crushed red pepper flakes
- Kosher salt, to taste
- Black pepper, to taste
- 4 basil leaves, torn into medium pieces

Method:

1. Mix olive oil, with lemon zest, red pepper flakes, salt, and black pepper in a bowl.
2. Rub this mixture over the zucchini slices liberally.
3. Turn the "Selector" knob to the "Grill Panini" side.
4. Preheat the bottom grill of Cuisine Griddler at 300 degrees F and the upper grill plate on medium heat.
5. Once it is preheated, open the lid and place the zucchini slices in the Griddler.
6. Close the griddler's lid and grill the zucchini for 5 minutes.
7. Garnish with basil leaves.
8. Serve.

Nutritional Information per Serving:

- Calories 138
- Total Fat 4.8 g
- Saturated Fat 1.7 g
- Cholesterol 12 mg
- Sodium 520 mg
- Total Carbs 5.3 g
- Fiber 2.3 g
- Sugar 1.2 g
- Protein 2.1 g

Veggie Burger

Preparation Time: 10 minutes
Cooking time: 5 minutes
Serving: 5

Ingredients:

- 1 cup cooked brown rice
- 1 cup raw walnuts, finely chopped
- 1/2 tablespoons avocado oil
- 1/2 medium white onion, diced
- 1 tablespoon chili powder
- 1 tablespoon cumin powder
- 1 tablespoon smoked paprika
- 1/2 teaspoons sea salt
- 1/2 teaspoons black pepper
- 1 tablespoon coconut sugar
- 1 ½ cups cooked black beans, drained
- 1/3 cup panko bread crumbs
- 4 tablespoons BBQ sauce

Method:

1. Add brown rice, walnuts, and all the veggies burger ingredients to a food processor.
2. Blend this mixture for 3 minutes then transfer to a bowl.
3. Make 5 patties out of this vegetable beans mixture.
4. Turn the "Selector" knob to the "Grill Panini" side.
5. Preheat the bottom grill of Cuisine Griddler at 350 degrees F and the upper grill plate on medium heat.
6. Once it is preheated, open the lid and place the veggie burgers in the Griddler.
7. Close the griddler's lid and grill the burgers for 5 minutes.
8. Serve warm.

Nutritional Information per Serving:

- Calories 213
- Total Fat 14 g
- Saturated Fat 8 g
- Cholesterol 81 mg
- Sodium 162 mg
- Total Carbs 23 g

- Fiber 0.7 g
- Sugar 19 g
- Protein 12 g

Chapter 9: Dessert Recipes

Grilled Apples

Preparation Time: 10 minutes
Cooking time: 7 minutes
Serving: 4

Ingredients:

- 2 firm tart-sweet apples, sliced
- 2 tablespoons butter, melted
- 2 tablespoons brown sugar
- 2 tablespoons white sugar
- 1 teaspoon cinnamon
- 1/4 teaspoon ginger
- 1/4 teaspoon nutmeg

Method:

1. Mix sugar with butter, ginger, nutmeg, and cinnamon in a bowl.
2. Turn the "Selector" knob to the "Grill Panini" side.
3. Preheat the bottom grill of Cuisine Griddler at 350 degrees F and the upper grill plate on medium heat.
4. Once it is preheated, open the lid and place the apple slices in the Griddler.
5. Close the griddler's lid and grill the apples for 7 minutes.
6. Drizzle cinnamon butter on top and serve.

Nutritional Information per Serving:

- Calories 319
- Total Fat 11.9 g
- Saturated Fat 1.7 g
- Cholesterol 78 mg
- Sodium 79 mg
- Total Carbs 14.8 g
- Fiber 1.1 g
- Sugar 8.3 g
- Protein 5 g

Rum-Soaked Pineapple

Preparation Time: 10 minutes
Cooking time: 14 minutes
Serving: 4

Ingredients:

- 1/2 cup rum
- 1/2 cup packed brown sugar
- 1 teaspoon ground cinnamon
- 1 pineapple, cored and sliced
- Vanilla ice cream

Method:

1. Mix run with cinnamon and brown sugar in a suitable bowl.
2. Pour this mixture over the pineapple rings and mix well.
3. Let them soak for 15 minutes and flip the pineapples after 7 minutes.
4. Turn the "Selector" knob to the "Grill Panini" side.
5. Preheat the bottom grill of Cuisine Griddler at 350 degrees F and the upper grill plate on medium heat.
6. Once it is preheated, open the lid and place the pineapple slices in the Griddler.
7. Close the griddler's lid and grill the pineapple for 5-7 minutes until lightly charred.
8. Serve with ice cream.

Nutritional Information per Serving:

- Calories 427
- Total Fat 31.1 g
- Saturated Fat 4.2 g
- Cholesterol 123 mg
- Sodium 86 mg
- Total Carbs 49 g
- Sugar 12.4 g
- Fiber 19.8 g
- Protein 13.5 g

Cinnamon Grilled Peaches

Preparation Time: 10 minutes
Cooking time: 2 minutes
Serving: 4

Ingredients:

- 1/4 cup salted butter
- 1 tablespoon 1 teaspoon granulated sugar
- 1/4 teaspoon cinnamon
- 4 ripe peaches, pitted and sliced

Method:

1. Mix sugar with butter and cinnamon in a bowl until smooth.
2. Turn the "Selector" knob to the "Grill Panini" side.
3. Preheat the bottom grill of Cuisine Griddler at 350 degrees F and the upper grill plate on medium heat.
4. Once it is preheated, open the lid and place the peach slices in the Griddler.
5. Close the griddler's lid and grill the peaches for 2 minutes.
6. Drizzle cinnamon butter on top and serve.

Nutritional Information per Serving:

- Calories 401
- Total Fat 8.9 g
- Saturated Fat 4.5 g
- Cholesterol 57 mg
- Sodium 340 mg
- Total Carbs 54.7 g
- Fiber 1.2 g
- Sugar 1.3 g
- Protein 5.3 g

Banana Butter Kabobs

Preparation Time: 10 minutes
Cooking time: 3 minutes
Serving: 6

Ingredients:

- 1 loaf (10 ¾ oz.) cake, cubed
- 2 large bananas, one-inch slices
- 1/4 cup butter, melted
- 2 tablespoons brown sugar
- 1/2 teaspoon vanilla extract
- 1/8 teaspoon ground cinnamon
- 4 cups butter pecan ice cream
- 1/2 cup butterscotch ice cream topping
- 1/2 cup pecans, chopped and toasted

Method:

1. Thread the cake and bananas over the skewers alternately.
2. Whisk butter with cinnamon, vanilla, and brown sugar in a small bowl.
3. Brush this mixture over the skewers liberally.
4. Turn the "Selector" knob to the "Grill Panini" side.
5. Preheat the bottom grill of Cuisine Griddler at 300 degrees F and the upper grill plate on medium heat.
6. Once it is preheated, open the lid and place the banana skewers in the Griddler.
7. Close the griddler's lid and grill the skewers for 3 minutes.
8. Serve with ice cream, pecan, and butterscotch topping on top.

Nutritional Information per Serving:

- Calories 419
- Total Fat 19.7 g
- Saturated Fat 18.6 g
- Cholesterol 141 mg
- Sodium 193 mg
- Total Carbs 23.7 g
- Fiber 0.9 g
- Sugar 19.3 g
- Protein 5.2 g

Marshmallow Stuffed Banana

Preparation Time: 10 minutes
Cooking time: 8 minutes
Serving: 1

Ingredients:

- ¼ cup of chocolate chips
- 1 banana
- ¼ cup mini marshmallows

Method:

1. Place a peeled banana over a 12 x 12-inch foil sheet.
2. Make a slit in the banana lengthwise and stuff this slit with chocolate chips and marshmallows.
3. Wrap the foil around the banana and seal it.
4. Turn the "Selector" knob to the "Griddle" side.
5. Prepare and preheat the bottom plate of Cuisine Griddler at 300 degrees F.
6. Once it is preheated, open the lid and place the banana in the Griddler.
7. Cook the banana in the Griddler for 4 minutes, flip and cook for another 4 minutes.
8. Unwrap and serve.

Nutritional Information per Serving:

- Calories 372
- Total Fat 11.8 g
- Saturated Fat 4.4 g
- Cholesterol 62 mg
- Sodium 871 mg
- Total Carbs 45.8 g
- Fiber 0.6 g
- Sugar 27.3 g
- Protein 4 g

Marshmallow Roll-Up

Preparation Time: 10 minutes
Cooking time: 5 minutes
Serving: 2

Ingredients:

- 1 flour tortilla
- 1 handful mini marshmallows
- 1 handful of chocolate chips
- 2 graham crackers

Method:

1. Spread a 12x12 inch foil on a working surface.
2. Place the tortilla over this sheet and top it with graham crackers, chocolate chips, and marshmallows.
3. Roll the tortilla tightly by rolling the foil sheet.
4. Turn the "Selector" knob to the "Grill Panini" side.
5. Preheat the bottom grill of Cuisine Griddler at 300 degrees F and the upper grill plate on medium heat.
6. Once it is preheated, open the lid and place the wraps in the Griddler.
7. Close the griddler's lid and grill the wraps for 5 minutes.
8. Unwrap and slice in half.
9. Serve.

Nutritional Information per Serving:

- Calories 495
- Total Fat 17.5 g
- Saturated Fat 4.8 g
- Cholesterol 283 mg
- Sodium 355 mg
- Total Carbs 26.4 g
- Fiber 1.8 g
- Sugar 0.8 g
- Protein 17.4 g

Fruit Kabobs

Preparation Time: 10 minutes
Cooking time: 9 minutes
Serving: 6

Ingredients:

- 1 tablespoon butter
- 1/2 cup apricot preserves
- 1 tablespoon water
- 1/8 teaspoon ground cinnamon
- 1/8 teaspoon ground nutmeg
- 3 nectarines, quartered
- 3 peaches, quartered
- 3 plums, quartered
- 1 loaf (10 ¾ oz.) lb. cake, cubed

Method:

1. Take the first five ingredients in a small saucepan and stir cook for 3 minutes on medium heat.
2. Alternately thread the lb. cake and fruits on the skewers.
3. Brush these skewers with the apricot mixture.
4. Turn the "Selector" knob to the "Grill Panini" side.
5. Preheat the bottom grill of Cuisine Griddler at 350 degrees F and the upper grill plate on medium heat.
6. Once it is preheated, open the lid and place the fruit skewers in the Griddler.
7. Close the griddler's lid and grill the skewers for 4-6 minutes until lightly charred.
8. Serve.

Nutritional Information per Serving:

- Calories 248
- Total Fat 15.7 g
- Saturated Fat 2.7 g
- Cholesterol 75 mg
- Sodium 94 mg
- Total Carbs 38.4 g
- Fiber 0.3 g
- Sugar 10.1 g
- Protein 14.1 g

Apricots with Brioche

Preparation Time: 10 minutes
Cooking time: 5 minutes
Serving: 4

Ingredients:

- 8 ripe apricots
- 2 tablespoon butter
- 2 tablespoon sugar
- 4 brioche slices
- 2 tablespoon Honey
- 2 cup vanilla ice cream

Method:

1. Toss the apricot halves with butter and sugar.
2. Turn the "Selector" knob to the "Grill Panini" side.
3. Preheat the bottom grill plate of Cuisine Griddler at 350 degrees F and the upper grill plate at medium heat.
4. Once it is preheated, open the lid and place the brioche slices in the Griddler.
5. Close the griddle's lid and grill the brioche for 3 minutes.
6. Transfer the grilled slices to a plate and keep them aside.
7. Now place the apricot slices in the Griddler, close the lid, and cook for 2 minutes.
8. Transfer the grilled apricots to the brioche slices and top with honey, sugar, and ice cream.
9. Serve.

Nutritional Information per Serving:

- Calories 398
- Total Fat 13.8 g
- Saturated Fat 5.1 g
- Cholesterol 200 mg
- Sodium 272 mg
- Total Carbs 53.6 g
- Fiber 1 g
- Sugar 1.3 g
- Protein 11.8 g

Conclusion

In every family, there is a personality that urges each member to look for activities outside the family. But most people will never forget to participate in common activities that strengthen family ties and enhance the sense of love. Having a Cuisinart Griddler cookbook will help you organize these activities better.

Cuisinart Griddler starter recipe 2021 will be your best choice whether you are cooking for one person or the whole family! Thank you for buying this book. Now start your gourmet journey!

www.ingramcontent.com/pod-product-compliance
Lightning Source LLC
Chambersburg PA
CBHW081404070526
44583CB00020B/2673